COMPILED AND EDITED BY
SUSAN CHEEVES KING

Broken Arrow, OK

Scripture quotations marked CEB are taken from the *Common English Bible*. Copyright © 2011 by Common English Bible. Nashville, Tennessee.

Scripture quotations marked ESV are taken from *The Holy Bible, English Standard Version*. ESV® Permanent Text Edition® (2016). Copyright © 2001 by Crossway Bibles, a publishing ministry of Good News Publishers. Used by pemission.

Scripture quotations marked KJV are taken from the *King James Version* of the Bible.

Scripture quotations marked MSG are taken from The Message Bible. Copyright © 1993, 1994, 1995, 1996, 2000, 2001, 2002 by Eugene H. Peterson

Scripture quotations marked NCV are taken from the *New Century Version*®. Copyright © 2005 by Thomas Nelson. Used by permission. All rights reserved.

Scripture quotations marked NKJV are taken from the *New King James Version*®. Copyright © 1982 by Thomas Nelson. Used by permission. All rights reserved.

Scripture quotations marked NIV are taken from the *The Holy Bible, New International Version*. Copyright © 1973, 1978, 1984, International Bible Society. Used by permission of Zondervan. All rights reserved.

Scripture quotations marked NRSV are taken from the *New Revised Standard Version Bible*, copyright © 1989 the Division of Christian Education of the National Council of the Churches of Christ in the United States of America. Used by permission. All rights reserved.

Short and Sweet Goes Fourth

ISBN-13: 978-1-60495-045-8

Copyright © 2018 by Susan Cheeves King. Published in the USA by Grace Publishing. All rights reserved. No part of this book may be reproduced in any form or by any electronic or mechanical means, including information storage and retrieval systems, without permission in writing, except as provided by USA Copyright law.

Table of Contents

Introduction 7
1. Write On *Karen Condit* 11
2. Max the Guard Dog *Craig Hodgins* 12
3. Stop, Thief! *Tabitha Abel* 14
4. To Tokyo with a Toddler *Lanita Bradley Boyd* 16
5. How Do I Love God? *Jeanetta Chrystie* 18
6. Kintsukuroi *Jorja Davis* 20
7. The Heart Knows *Andrea Woronick* 22
8. While in This Skin *Tina M. Hunt* 24
9. Adopted by God *Leslie Neal Segraves* 25
10. Fight for Your Life *Karma Pratt* 27
11. The Sea *Doris Hoover* 30
12. Wait *Pat Gerbrandt* 32
13. Found *Karen deBlieck* 33
14. A Mop Pail, Water Holes, and a Shared Smile
    Pamela Groupe Groves 36
15. The Burning Bin *Jewell Utt* 38
16. A Gift From My Mom *Susanna Shutz Robar* 40
17. All Now Brought Near *Frank Ramirez* 42
18. When I Need to Get Away *Troy Dennis* 43
19. To Plant a Seed in West Africa *Reba Rhyne* 45
20. Beauty and the Least *Patricia Huey* 47
21. Santa in the Kush *Jack Scott Stanley* 49
22. Why I Love Big Papa *Michelle Ruschman* 51
23. Diary 1965 *Dottie Lovelady Rogers* 53
24. Frenzy to Fancy *Sharon Atwood* 55
25. Dirge for a Pipe Organ *Karen O. Allen* 57
26. Hope *Karen Woodard* 59
27. The Best Place on Earth *Sharon Cook* 61
28. Soles *E.V. Sparrow* 63
29. In the Beginning *Karis Waller* 65

30. BREAD *Karis Waller* 66
31. THE STACK OF BOOKS *Adora (Jenny) Calvert* 67
32. MY CHILD HAS A CHILD *Shelley Pierce* 69
33. THE HEART OF GOD *Adam Benson* 71
34. WORLD REACH *Alice H. Murray* 73
35. A GENTLE ANSWER *Lauren Craft* 74
36. LOVE AT FIRST SIGHT *Jeff Adams* 76
37. THE LAST VERSE *Joanne Fleck* 78
38. DON'T DRINK THAT – DON'T EAT THIS *Michelle Walker-Wade* 80
39. HOPE DURING A TOUGH YEAR *Carol Harrison* 82
40. SISTER *Leah Hinton* 84
41. TO LYNDELL WITH LOVE *Tony Roberts* 86
42. G G *Debbie Pierce* 88
43. FOR THE SAKE OF CHRIST *Kay Marshall Strom* 90
44. SLOW, SURE STEPS *Jon Drury* 93
45. WHY IS HE STILL HERE? *Sharon Fincannon* 94
46. VALID ID *Suzanne D. Nichols* 96
47. LAST ACT *Marcia Lee Laycock* 97
48. DOWN THE STREET *Sheila Humphrey* 99
49. HANNAH'S SON *Carol Schafer* 101
50. THE CALL OF THE BEACH *Sue Rosenfeld* 103
51. THE ACHE TO BE WHOLE *Liz Kimmel* 104
52. THE BIG DATE *Bob LaForge* 106
53. THIS TIME *Mary Lou Redding* 108
54. IS THAT GOD? *Lin Daniels* 110
55. The Un-Contemplatable *Paul Hinton* 112
56. MY BOY *Wilma R. Vernich* 114
57. IN HIS BOOK *Becky Hitchcock* 115
58. RESCUE AT THE TELE-WINK GRILL *Kenneth Avon White* 117
59. QUILTS AND MORE QUILTS *Patricia A. Earl* 119
60. MAYBE NEXT TIME *Mary Hunt Webb* 121
61. FAITH, LOVE, MUSIC *Marcy O'Rourke* 123
ABOUT THE AUTHORS 125

INTRODUCTION

It all started decades ago when Mary Lou Redding caught an idea from a professor at Fort Wayne University. Further inspired by Joseph A. Ecclesine's "Big Words Are for the Birds" (at the end of the Introduction), she started assigning a one-syllable-word exercise in classes she taught at various writers' conferences all over the country.

Over the past twenty years, I have continued giving this assignment to those in my own classes. Writers at these conferences are motivated to learn whatever I can teach them about perfecting their craft because they know they're going to apply what they've learned, probably within an hour after they leave the classroom.

Still, they have come with the attitude that we who love to write all share. After all, we're writers. We love words. If a few words are good, many are better — especially the interesting word, maybe the elegant word…and definitely the special word only a particular writer can use.

And we do love to use the long, impressive words. But that can work against good communication. The truth is, the best communication is what the readers/listeners understand with the least effort — a Mr. Spock mind meld as it were — as if the ideas are just flowing from the writer's mind to theirs with no actual words involved.

We may love words, but if we use too many of them and ones that are not familiar and comfortable to the average reader/listener, then words just get in the way. Writing tight (saying a lot with a little) and using crisp, clear, accessible words in our writing and speech bring joy to the readers/listeners even if they may not know why.

That's good news for any of us who long for others to understand us, to hear us. The words we really should be using most of the time are already known to us. We don't have to get a college degree to learn them; we just think that we do. So we all need to break our attachments to those multi-syllable aliens that even non-professional writers/speakers tend to favor and get back to the simple words of our childhood.

Here is the assignment the writers in this book were given:

Choose something you're passionate about, something that's important to you. Then write about it in 250-550 words, using words of only one syllable. We are accepting non-fiction, fiction, and poetry submissions.

Six exceptions:

1. Any proper noun is okay. (Don't lie. If you were born in California, don't write Maine; if a name is *Machenheimer*, don't write *Clark*.)
2. You may use polysyllabic words of 5 letters or fewer — for example: *into, over, area, about*
3. You may use contractions of more than one syllable such as *couldn't, wouldn't, didn't*
4. You may use numbers (even those that are polysyllabic).
5. As in any published work, direct quotes must be rendered word-for-word as they appear in the original, so their wording is exempt from the rules. This includes verses from the Bible — but only translations, not paraphrases (such as *The Message*).
6. Words for family (for which there are no one-syllable synonyms) are fine: *mother, father, sister, brother, sibling, husband, daughter, cousin, nephew, family.*

If you're a writer — or aspire to be — and this assignment intrigues you, why not give it a try? If you contact me at shortandsweettoo@gmail.com, I will send you the upcoming theme. You could be seeing your own work featured in the next book in the *Short and Sweet* series.

Susan Cheeves King

Big Words Are for the Birds
Joseph A. Ecclesine

When you come right down to it, there is no law that says you have to use big words in ads.

There are lots of small words, and good ones, that can be made to say all the things you want to say — quite as well as the big ones.

It may take more time to find the small words — but it can be well worth it. For most small words are quick to grasp. And best of all, most of us know what they mean.

Some small words — a lot of them, in fact — can say a thing just the way it should be said. They can be crisp, brief, to the point. Or they can be soft, round, smooth — rich with just the right feel, the right taste.

Use them with care and what you say can be slow or fast to read — as you wish.

Small words have a charm all their own — the charm of the quick, the lean, the lithe, the light on their toes. They dance, twist, turn, sing — light the way for the eyes of those who read, like sparks in the night — and stay on to sing some more.

Small words are clean, the grace notes of prose. There is an air to them that leaves you with the keen sense that they could not be more clear.

You know what they say the way you know a day is bright and fair — at first sight. And you find as you read that you like the way they say it.

Small words are sweet — to the ear, the tongue, and the mind.

Small words are gay — and lure you to their song as the flame lures the moth (which is not a bad thing for an ad to do).

Small words have a world of their own — a big world in which all of us live most of the time (which makes it a good place for ads, too).

And small words can catch big thoughts and hold them up for all who read to see — like bright stones in rings of gold.

With a good stock of small words, and the will to use them, you can write ads that will do all you want your ads to do — and more, much more.

In fact, if you play your cards right, you can write ads the way they all say ads should be done: in words like these (all the way down to the last one, that is) of just one syllable.

About Joseph A. Ecclesine

Joseph A. Ecclesine was a Madison Avenue copywriter in the *Mad Men* era. He originally wrote this piece in the 1960s for other copywriters.

A shorter version titled "Words of One Syllable," ran in *Reader's Digest*.

These two versions have also appeared in various other publications while being used as inspirational models for college writing courses around the country.

Born in Boston, Ecclesine graduated from Fordham University in 1929, months before the stock market crash that triggered the Great Depression. He was fortunate to find work at the *Bronx Home News* during that period. He later worked in the press department of NBC in Manhattan, where he met his future wife, Margy, also a writer there.

They celebrated more than 50 years of marriage and had eight children. While living in New York, he worked at several major ad agencies and became promotion director of *Look Magazine*.

His catchy headlines and prose could be found in the campaigns of numerous companies, including IBM, National Geographic, Revlon and American Airlines. He also wrote fiction and essays, with a 1930s piece in *Esquire* magazine, followed by work in *The New Yorker, Newsweek* and *Short Story International*. He had an innate curiosity about everything, which translated into an extreme zest for life.

An accomplished watercolorist, Ecclesine allegedly sold his first piece to boxer Gene Tunney, who held the world heavyweight championship in the late 1920s. Ecclesine's watercolors were featured in *The Artist* magazine, and he had a one-man show during his retirement in San Diego. While living in California during his final years, he taught courses in memoir writing for senior citizens in a continuing education program at UCSD (University of California at San Diego).

1
WRITE ON

Eve slammed the rest of the mail on the chair. "I've had it! I give up!"

She read the words that had crushed her more than once: *It's not right for us. We wish you the best.*

She'd been asked to send the first three parts of her novel. She thought this her best chance yet. Her hopes were high. She had poured her heart out for years on this dream.

Then she let it out, "At least they could sign their name! I mean — how long does that take?"

Her four-year-old son heard her and came out of his room. "Mom?" Jake had been by the side of his mom's desk ever since his first weeks of life. As a baby, he would coo while she read fresh words from her pen. As he grew, he would play with toys and look at books. Now he would kneel with his crayons on the chair next to hers and say, "I'm a writer, too."

"They don't like my book," she said.

Jake leaned in and hugged her waist. "I do."

Tears leaked and ran down Eve's cheeks. She sat down like a rag doll. "I'm done with this," she sighed.

As she stared at the floor, Jake left the room.

When he came back he stood in front of her. He raised his crayon sign. Faint lines and curves made the words that were framed on her desk. He could not read yet, but he had watched his mom stare at these words more than once: *Keep Calm and Write On.*

Eve pulled her son in and kissed the top of his head. "Let's have lunch. We've got work to do."

Karen Condit

2
MAX THE GUARD DOG

We once had a dog named Max. Part Australian Shepherd and part German Shepherd, Max was huge. As he stood on his hind legs, front paws on each side of my neck, Max could stretch to over five feet tall.

Since he was born the alpha male, he thought he was the boss. He would bite, growl, and try to herd us. After we paid a man to train him, Max grew to be a good dog.

If we had folks over for an event, he thought they had come to visit him, not us. He greeted each guest at the door with a

MAX AND CRAIG'S SON, MICHAEL

smile and a wag of his curly tail. Max was an image of God's total love for each one of us.

Max loved to be out in the yard, where we would play ball or have him chase a stick. When the game was done, and all was quiet, Max would trot the edge of our yard and then stretch out on the grass to keep guard over us.

Each night our son Michael would pet the dog and say, "Good night, Max." And each new day Max would be there to lick Michael as he lay in his bed, as if to tell him that it was time to get up. Max loved to lick – hands, feet, face, even ears. All were okay with him.

But all good things must end. On a wet spring night, our meek-yet-jolly giant had a stroke. His once-strong frame, now weak, lay spread on the floor. The light that once shone in his eyes was now dim — but not yet spent. For Max was not done; he had one more task to do. All at once he stood and moved to the back door. I let him out, and he began to pace the length of the fence, as if on guard duty once again. He made one final round and then he lay down on the cool grass in the rain. There, Max the guard dog went to sleep one last time.

We laid him to rest in a grave near the back shed, where he still keeps watch over us to this day.

Craig Hodgins

FICTION

3
STOP, THIEF!

Friends at church won't be happy with me, Harriet mused, *but I'm tired of being told I must sit still for this or that just 'cuz I'm a Christian. Didn't Jesus put some mean folk in their place? Didn't He turn over the tables of those lying cheats in His Father's House — twice? He showed up the scribes' and Pharisees' greed too, when He said that the money they flashed was worth less than the widow's two mites. Maybe I did the right thing, after all.*

Harriet had been a good child and was never mean or sassy at school. Her parents had taught her right from wrong, and she still went to church every week. She worked as a nurse – a sweet nurse, not bossy and loud as some are. She felt her clients' pain, and if she couldn't cure them, she'd cheer them up and then go home and pray for them.

She took a sip of tea and thought through the whole event.

Late out from work, she had dashed to the store to get eggs, a small block of cheese, and a bar of soap. With no cart, she grabbed and ran — sort of — up and down the aisles. She'd pay cash and get out in no time.

Her luck did not stop at the check-out. The lady in front of her had just paid for her three bags of goods. Harriet put her stuff on the belt, but as she did so a $20 bill fell from her purse to the floor. She bent to pick it up only to see the lady in front of her grab it.

Harriet smiled at her.

"Thanks," she said as she put out her hand, only to see the lady stuff Harriet's $20 in her own purse.

"That's mine," Harriet said.

"What's on the earth, goes to she who finds it," the woman said as she started for the exit.

Harriet was shocked.

For the first time in her life, Harriet put aside her be-nice-to-all mind-set and made a bee-line for the door. She rushed after the thief and caught her by her car where the wrong key was stuck in the lock. She had put her stuff down by the trunk to try to pull the key out.

Quick as a flash, Harriet grabbed the three bags and ran.

"What's on the earth, goes to she who finds it," Harriet yelled as she rushed off.

She threw the bags onto the front seat and flew for the exit. *Great — no blue lights.*

It was not like her to steal. Her heart fell as she warred with a tug of pride that she had shown a real thief that the Ten Commandments were still fair. *No one like that should mess with me or any Christian*, she thought, *just 'cuz she can.*

Safe to say, it wasn't God. Was it karma? She didn't know. At that time all she knew was that she had three pounds of fresh river trout, a *large* block of cheese, a big bag of grapes, a pecan pie — and more, much more.

As Harriet sipped her tea, she planned that she would take the extra food to the church. She still wasn't sure that she would tell them the story. But she was sure that God does take care of real-live Christians who are not door-mats, even Harriet.

Tabitha Abel

4
TO TOKYO WITH A TODDLER

"No, I'm sorry. There's no way I can put you four people in seats together. Maybe when you get on the plane you can talk someone into changing seats," the Northwest Airline desk clerk said. My son, Josh, and his wife, Gina, looked at each other, shocked. Their seats were all over the plane.

"But one of our seats is for our thirteen-month-old!" Gina cried, with Kinley in her arms. "We can't sit in four different places!" The clerk turned away. Kelsey, Josh's sister, the third adult on the Let's Start Talking mission team, joined the sad parents. They found a place in the Minneapolis International Airport to pray. And pray. And plan. And pray.

"I don't think I can handle Kinley by myself all the way to Thailand — even if I can get someone to swap," Gina moaned. "Maybe my dad was right when he said it was crazy to take a baby on a six-week mission trip to Thailand."

They got to board first since they had a young child with them. They looked about the huge plane to find four seats that would work well for them on this 12-hour flight from Minneapolis to Tokyo.

"Let's sit in these four in the front row," Gina said. "That way Kinley can have a bit more space to move around." They sat down and braced themselves to ask the people who would claim these seats if they would spread about the plane in the other four seats.

The plane didn't seem to be filled, but still they had closed the doors. The four team mates looked at each other, shocked. No one had claimed their seats! They spoke to the woman in charge.

"Actually, the ones who had these seats missed their flight," she said. "You're good to go!"

The team talked about the fate of the four who had planned a big trip to Tokyo and then missed their flight. They felt blessed but also sad for the folks who were stuck in Minneapolis.

Then they heard the captain: "Ladies and gentlemen, I'm sorry, but we're going to have to turn back to the gate. There is a minor equipment difficulty that must be remedied before we depart."

While the plane was being fixed, the four who had missed the flight came and were able to board. They were thrilled to make their flight after all.

"Since you are late, just find an empty seat and take it," the flight attendant said. They found the team's four empty seats and didn't mind that their seats were not in the same row. They were just glad to be on the plane.

The three adults praised God for being so blessed. Even though they had prayed that the seats would work out, they would never have dreamed they could all sit in the same row.

Daughter Kelsey, son Josh, Daughter-in-law Gina holding their daughter, Kinley

"God is so good!" Gina cried.

"Talk about doing 'immeasurably more than all we ask or imagine!'" said Josh.

"Yes, He even eased our guilt when those others got on board after all," Kelsey said. "Now if He'll just keep Kinley quiet for the next twelve hours...."

Lanita Bradley Boyd

5
How Do I Love God?

Jesus said, "'Love the Lord your God with all your heart and with all your soul and with all your strength and with all your mind'; and, 'Love your neighbor as yourself.'"

Luke 10:27 NIV

How do I love God with all of my heart, soul, mind, and strength? What does that mean? Where do I start? What do I do to love God — say "I love you" and then go on about my day? No, there must be more to it. So I asked God, "How do I love you like that?"

As I seek to break this verse into parts, to grasp its full worth, I jot down bits of thoughts to help them jell. A pure heart. A clear mind. He is my strength. The Holy Spirit brings verse after verse to my mind.

To love God with all of my heart, I need a pure heart. I need to pray for God to cleanse me of my sins and give me a clean heart.

To love God with all of my mind, I need a clear mind and a clean mind. A clear mind would focus on the tasks at hand. A clean mind would not be full of junk. I need to trust God to help me choose what to watch and what to read. I need to bathe my mind in His Word daily and take time to learn from it.

To love God with all of my strength, I guess I need to be strong. But what does that mean? I think about the lack of strength in my frame; I am more weak than strong in that sense. The Holy Bible says the "joy of the Lord is my strength" so could it be that it means strength of will? Yes, that sounds right. I need to let God be my strength of will in each choice I make.

Soul — now that is a tough one. I have heard that our soul has three parts: my mind, my will, and all that I feel. I think I see; I am to love God with all my parts. My heart is what I feel and what I care about; my strength of will is based in God, and my mind is bathed in God's Word. Then I can love God with all my heart, mind, and strength — which makes up my soul.

Then, the verse adds one more way to love God: to love those He loves.

This small Bible verse is full of deep thoughts. The gist of it is to love God with all that is me. The crux of it is that to love God is not a thing of ease; it calls for a shift in how I live each day. The meat of it is that I am to grow into a child of God who can love God as He wants to be loved!

Jeanetta Chrystie

FICTION

6

Kintsukuroi
(keen-tsoo-koo-roy)

The young man formed tea bowl after tea bowl after tea bowl. Glazed and fired, each new bowl he brought to the Master Potter's wheel.

The Japanese Master closed his eyes and felt the bowl with his gnarled hands. Then he used his eyes. He turned the tea bowl this way and that in the light. He gave it to the young man to do the same. In so doing, they found at least one small flaw. This way the young man learned. He bowed to his tutor and took the bowl back to put on the shelf above his wheel. He took his wire, then cut and began to knead another lump of clay, to start a new bowl.

Then, one day, in the far back of the kiln, it came to be. The clay was thin and even. The glaze did not have even one purl — a tea bowl to be placed on the tray of a Samurai. He rushed to the Master, who raised the bowl to the light. It was black, yet the light shone through. With his stiff hands, he felt the clay and the glaze, inside and out. He gave the bowl to the young man.

"A fine tea bowl, my son. the Master spoke in a soft voice. "I can make none as well." Then he paused to say, "Now, drop the bowl on the floor."

The young man felt his face flush. His eyes filled with tears. His heart felt torn and heavy. With his back straight, he sank to his knees. His pride turned end over end as the cup fell from his hands.

At first it bounced, and then he heard it break. It was as if the earth had split and crushed the young man's soul.

"Open the bag," the Master said.

The Master dropped low from his stool and knelt with care.

The young man watched as the old man began to pick up the broken bowl. Into the open bag, he slipped the shards of the bowl — the bowl that once had no flaws. The young man closed the bag and then stood still and mute.

"And now," said the Master, "we will make your bowl so that it will be a high gift for a Daimyo or even the Mikado."

The two sat side by side. They mixed resin with fine ground gold and began to glue the shards of the bowl together. Once a tea bowl with no flaw, so fine the light could shine through, it now was veined with strength. Its gold scars had turned it into a gift of great worth, fit for a baron — or even the Emperor.

Jorja Davis

Kintsukuroi – Japanese for "golden mend" or "to repair with gold"

Image courtesy
of Morty Bachar,
Lakeside Pottery studio
www.lakesidepottery.com

Image courtesy
of Morty Bachar,
Lakeside Pottery studio
www.lakesidepottery.com

7
THE HEART KNOWS

As I walked down the hall at the Alzheimer's home, I looked in the room next to my mom's where an old man lay still in his bed, his eyes fixed on the wall in front of him. It was ten o'clock, and I knew that his wife would be there soon. She had a slow gait, and a large bag hung on her arm. I watched as she walked to his room.

Each day would be the same. She would pause at his door, walk in, set her bag down, and stand close to his bed. She then took hold of the sheets and made sure that he was tucked in. She reached out and fixed his hair with her frail hand, leaned down, and gave him a soft kiss on his cheek. Next, she sat on the chair by his bed and looked at him as she took three things from her tote; a book, her yarn, and a brown lunch bag. She read to him, sang to him, and talked to him. She spoke of the warm sun, the cool winds, her bus ride there, and the news of the day. She hummed as she knit, and then closed her eyes for a short nap. At lunch time, she would feed him and then bring the straw to his lips, so he could sip some milk. He gave no sign that he knew who she was, no way to show if he heard her words, and yet, that did not stop her. Her love knew no bounds.

And then one day she did not come. I asked the nurse where she was and was told that she had passed. I watched as the nurse went to the man's room, fixed the sheets, brushed his hair and smiled at him. Did he know that it was not the same? Did he know that it was not his wife who was with him? I had no way to be sure; his face did not change, his eyes stayed fixed on the wall. I felt that it was good he did not know. When the nurse left, I walked to the door and glanced in at him. My heart sank, for on his cheek I saw a tear. He knew. He knew that she was gone.

The next day, I was not in a rush to get there. I was sad for it was the end of the love song that I had watched these past months. The nurse did her best to care for him but could not match his wife's love and care.

Then one day, when I went to see my mom, I saw that he was not there. A nurse told me that he had died. I paused, closed my eyes, and smiled. The love that they shared in this life will live on in the next; I had no doubt. And now, I know that his eyes are not fixed on that wall in front of him; they are fixed on her.

Andrea Woronick

8
WHILE IN THIS SKIN

God paid a great price for you.
So while in your skin, make sure you bless God.

Author's paraphrase of 1 Corinthians 6:20

I trust that this verse is true, but I don't tend to live it to the full. I eat the wrong foods — at the wrong times. I sit too much. I fail to aim at a fit life. At my last check-up, I was told once more how much joy and health I miss due to my choice not to live and do what I know.

When I think on this, I shake my head and want to cry. What have I done? I used to work at Curves. I taught ways to eat right and how to be fit. I *know* what to do. I just don't do it.

'til now!

A friend has lost a lot of weight, and I asked her how. She's now my coach. I share with her each week how I've done, then make plans for how to go on. I joined a group of folks with like minds. We share our joys and cheer each one on to our goals. When I join with those who seek good health, I can find that the strength to reach my goals is in my reach.

Best of all: the pounds fall off, and my pep is back.

I see now how much more joy I have with God. He made this sack of bones and gave it to me as a gift. He loves me so much He gave His son to buy me back from sin.

One way I can say thanks is to choose to take care of *me*. I am made by God. I must take care of this great gift.

When I choose to eat good food to fuel this frame and choose not to laze through my days, I bless God. I say thanks. I have JOY!

Tina M. Hunt

9
ADOPTED BY GOD

I chose to fast until the time would come that I heard the Lord's voice. I craved to know God's plan. On the fourth day, I sat and read through the book of John. I pled with the Lord for His will about what we had asked: *Should we bring a child from China into our home?*

At one point as I read through John, I stopped, looked up, and said, "Lord, I want to know your heart. Please help us! We don't know what to do!" I looked back down at the page, and my eyes fell upon these words, *"I will not leave you as orphans. I will come to you."* (John 14:18 NIV).

My heart skipped a beat. My eyes grew wide. My mind raced.

From that point on, our path was clear. We were to bring a girl out of China.

We had asked God for three things for our new daughter: 1. That she would be young. 2. That she would be in a Chinese home until we came. 3. That she would be from a place with no chance to hear the Good News of Jesus. God said yes to all three. She was 15 months old when we picked her up. From day two, she stayed in a home with three girls and a Chinese mom and dad. She is from the *most* lost part of China.

Three years ago, we went to her and she came to us.

This past April, we went to visit the ones who cared for Phoebe those 15 months. Though our child can't speak well due to her cleft lip and cleft in the roof of her mouth, she loves to talk and brings joy to our family while we serve in Asia. As we walked to her Chinese home, I said into her ear, "We will see your Chinese house, and then we will go back home. You are mine! We pray for a chance to share Jesus with them." As soon as she heard me say "Jesus," she said, "I tell them, mom!" As soon as she saw them, she ran to them and — with bright eyes — said, "Jesus and the cross!"

Later in a café, we sat to eat Chinese food alone in a room all our own. The mom and dad were there, their daughter-in-law and grandson, and their adopted daughter. Also there was one to speak English into Chinese and back into English for us. After the meal, Phoebe and the grandson were playing in the background as the rest of us talked, laughed, and shared life. Then a chance came to talk about Jesus. As we spoke, the mother showed an open heart and mind to Truth. In the midst of our talk, Phoebe ran to her and said, "I love you, foster mom. Thank you, foster mom." Those in the room heard and watched. God watched. God led. God moved.

Through our daughter, a family in this most-lost part of China heard the Good News. We placed a Book into their hands. Though this husband and wife were over 60 years old, this was the first time they had held God's Word and heard the Good News.

As we shared the story of Jesus with them, we saw that their hearts were soft. The mother would often pause and think. At one point, she asked, "Is Jesus God or a man?" Later, she said, "What you say makes sense. This is a good story. I like it. I will think on it more."

God loves the world. But the Good News is not good if it does not get there in time. Yet, this time, through the pain and scars of our child and Jesus, God made us able to share His grace, hope, and peace with a Chinese home. God has not left us "as orphans" but has come to us. In turn, may we each go to the world to share the news that Jesus has come to all!

Leslie Neal Segraves

10
Fight for Your Life

The Devil wants you dead.
'likes to mess with your head.
He'll steal your mind, your heart, your time,
Your soul, your love, your life.
He will take it all if you don't stand guard.

Jesus says,
"The thief comes only to steal and kill and destroy.
I came that they may have life and have it abundantly"
John 10:10 (NRSV).

"They" is you, dear child.
"They" is all who hold true to the good news.

God calls you
to a life lived fully and well.

It's about time —
To shape your soul.
Time to dive in, to dwell in the Lord,
Sink into His Word,
Sail through storms
Like a ship on the sea.
Don't fret about
The size of the waves
Or the means for the way.
The Lord will take care of each day.

"How do you know?"
"He told me so."

Faith looks strange
To those who don't know it.
Can't let that slow you down, though.

The Devil counts on fear
To slow
The steady stream of life
That flows
in your veins.

Dig in. Dive in.
Dwell. Bloom. Grow.
Be a light.

Show the world
what God looks like.

Let your heart be pruned,
Your soul be shaped,
The change take root.

*"The Lord God has put his Spirit in me,
because the Lord has appointed me
to tell the good news to the poor.
He has sent me to comfort those whose hearts are broken,
to tell the captives they are free,
and to tell the prisoners they are released"*
Isaiah 61:1 (NCV).

"They" is you.
You get to go, too.
You've made a break
from the walls that held you.
The blood of Christ is in you.
He makes a way,
and love breaks through.

God's heart for you shapes your faith.
As your face tilts up
To bask in the glory
Of the light of the Lord.

"It's about time," God says. "You saw the ways I am
    at work in you.
The Devil wants you dead, but I brought you
    back to life."

Called by name
Known by heart
"They" is you.

Karma Pratt

11

THE SEA

The sea — it calls to me. With swish and sway, ebb and flow, with in–and-out waves, it calls my name.

The song of the sea is a *lap-lap* tune that calms my mind. As waves wash the sand with notes of hope, fresh thoughts flow in and change my life. The sea breathes out air salt-sweet and clean. Its breath skims the shoals and blows through my heart with sighs of peace.

DORIS ON THE BEACH

At times, the sea roars like a fierce beast. It spews wild waves that slash the shore; yet I have no fear. My soul stays at rest. For in the waves, I glimpse the Lord's might; and I know that the One who rules the sea holds my life in His hands.

By day, the sun casts jewels on the sea. They dance with the sway of the tide. At night, the moon lays a path that links the earth to the stars, a lane of light that glows from sky to sea.

Where the sea and sky meet, the sun makes its bed. This is a place of spun-silk dreams, a place where prayers glow red, pink, and gold.

When I'm sad, my tears add depth to the swells. But the Lord sees my tears. He hears my cry. With salt air, he dries my cheeks and says, "Don't fret, child. All is well."

I'm loved by a God whose care is as deep and wide as the sea. His love spills out from my soul and dots the waves with flecks of joy.

This vast pool of water is my place of prayer, an open-air altar where I meet with the Lord. Here I stroll the edge of the sea, and hand in hand, Jesus walks with me.

I will never roam far. No, I must stay near, for the sea — it calls to me.

Doris Hoover

FICTION

12

WAIT

I sit in my chair and wait. No one comes to visit. I wait for friends who can't come. I wait for a face I know. I wait for food. I wait for a bath. The days are so long, and I tire of it all. I wait for night, for sleep. I long for ease. The pain grows, and aches do not fade.

I don't wait for pain or loss. They creep near each day — as my knees ache, and my hands can't hold the spoon for the pain.

"She won't eat."

I reach for a book, but it is hard to hold it up, to turn the page. When I try to read, my eyes dim, the words swim, and soon I sleep.

And then comes a voice at the edge of my sleep. Who is it? I see a shape, and then I see you. You say my name – too loud – but who are you? Ah…my…my…

Oh, I know your face but I do not know how to tell you!

Do you know what I need? I need you to hold me in your arms. I need to hear you. Sing to me; sing for me. If you can't sing, won't you pray? Do you think of this? I guess not; you want to go.

Don't just walk away! I'm still here! Will you come back? How long must I wait?

> *I will look to the LORD; I will wait for the God of my salvation;*
> *my God will hear me.*

Micah 7:7 ESV

Come for me; You will not be late! Be still, my heart, and wait. The light fades…

Pat Gerbrandt

13
FOUND

You did not walk to the water
And find me in the reeds,

Nor did You breathe
me into this world.

I did not grow into a small C
Curled snug and warm in Your womb.

Not mother
Brother
Father Sister
Child

You met me when I was a girl firm
But
with cracks and holes
Cruel dug into my skin
Blood not dry
Tears fresh.

How could You see past the scars
To the small bloom
A face that longs for the sun,
A weak spark,
Soft touch,
Meek words?

You brought me to heal,
And soon many came
Bent
Bruised

One by one we met —
Ripped scraps of cloth
No two the same
But to You
Each hue a joy.

You placed us
Frayed edge against frayed
To form a stitched quilt
Bound by You
Whole.

We are one.

Twined cords grow strong;
Roots run deep.

On tip toes, we grasp the dark night
While strong hands hold us up
To the stars

To Reach.

Our joy sings in the breeze
Lights up the night
Calls to the world —

Come!

Here, we are born again
Here, we curl up on Your chest
Your Holy breath on our cheek
To wake
And know that Here
is where we need to be.

Not built with roof or nail.
There is no hearth
No bed to lie our head.

We are bound by love
By hope.

We longed for it
And found it
Mid the shards of life
In You

Home

Karen deBlieck

14
A Mop Pail, Water Holes, and a Shared Smile

A few weeks prior to the day I turned five, my mom was busy using the string mop on our large floor. As she put the mop in the metal pail, I tugged on her blue capri pants for the third time to ask if I could help. She told me to go and see if the new family down the block had a girl who could play with me. The sound of rain told me I would need my lemon-color coat. I would also need my red boots for the dirt and rock road that had lots of holes filled with water.

As I strolled down the block, my feet found their way into every water hole I saw — as did a few rocks I'd picked up on the way. When I got to the house owned by folks I didn't know, I rang the bell and stood very still. A tall lady with a stern face came to the door. "Do you have a girl who can play with me?" I asked her. The lady said, "Yes I do, but she can't play today." From the back of her mother's long, full skirt, a girl with wild, curly, rosy blond hair and green eyes full of life peeked at me. The girl and I gave each other a bit of a smile, but we didn't have time to say a word. In a flash, the mother shut the door. Even so, I left happy. I had found a friend.

PAM LEFT BECKIE RIGHT -AT AGE 7

Today, close to 62 years later, I look back on my first stroll down the block to Beckie's house and see God's hand in my life. The green eyes so full of life I had seen that first day were a hint of the bright ideas and life story we would share. When we were six years old, we loved water. Why did Beckie's dad need a place just to park his car and keep his tools? Why couldn't we fill up that space with water from wall to wall so we could have a place to swim? Some of the water went out under the door, so we just left the hose on to fill it up while we went to eat lunch at my house. I never did hear what her dad thought of our plan.

At ten years old we found that Rose City Cemetery near my house spurred lots of ideas. We felt sorry for the graves that had no blossoms, so we "shared" some of the blossoms from the other graves. Some days we sprawled on the grass and ate our lunch. We used the lawn to run races and do stunts among the graves.

On that rainy, mop-pail day so long ago, God gave us the start of a bond that we would need to see us through the joy-filled and tough times of life. My granddaughter Marissa made that real to me when once she burst out with, "It's just like you and Beckie to keep doing things as a team." I had just told Marissa that Beckie had just found out she has cancer. I had begun a walk to treat cancer. We are the team God formed on the day of water holes and a smile.

PAM LEFT BECKIE RIGHT TODAY

Pamela Groupe Groves

15
THE BURNING BIN

I love the times, in years past, when my whole family went away to Corolla, North Carolina. Beach-house time was so much fun, so we worked hard for it. My siblings and I planned a family week, every year, when our kids were small. We would laugh, swim in the ocean, play on the beach, and eat. Each family was in charge of a main meal with sweets and Bible time, for the whole group, for one day. So we all had six days free. After we would eat and clean up, the kids would go out to play, while the adults had a time of prayer. At these times, my dad was so proud to see how much his whole family loved God.

The vacation home

One night, with hands held and heads bowed, we heard a noise that stopped our prayer — the ping of rocks on the front glass. We opened our eyes to a huge blaze and a crowd of cops, kids, and friends who waved us to come down to the street below.

Shocked by our plight, we went to see what's up. July 4th was coming up, and the older kids had bought flares to set off at dark.

When that fun was done, they placed them on top of a huge trash bin, then came in to play games. They thought the flares were out, but they were quite wrong. Still very hot, the flares had set the bin on fire. The tops of the flames reached up to the second floor where we stood in prayer. Though we didn't see the blaze at first, others had, and they phoned the cops. After the fire was put out, the bin looked like a flat piece of art.

My good friend owned this large beach house, and it fit our large family, so we drove there each year. We never before had an issue, but we were going to have to call her about this fire. So, we came up with a long story about a break in. Big bad thieves had robbed us at gun point and wreaked havoc in her house. We thought they were on drugs since they seemed to focus only on money. But then they fled away fast. We tried real hard to catch them but failed.

Then, with our last breath we said, "But don't you worry! We are all okay now. And we were able to clean up the whole mess. Oh, but for the trash can. It was burned to the ground. Darn thieves!"

Since she has known our tribe for years, this story came as no shock to her. She laughed at our joke and said, "I'll send you the bill for the can." We said, "Okay" and went on to enjoy the rest of our stay. Time away with family can be great fun!

Jewell Utt

16
A Gift From My Mom

A gift from the heart of a friend or kin is worth more than gold. My mom taught me that when I was young. It could be a gift to touch, see, and use. Or it could be seen only through the eyes of the soul. I saw my mom give gifts like that: of her time, her skill, or her soft, calm air. She would make a phone call, drop in on a friend with a pot of hot soup and a fresh loaf of bread, send a card. She would pen words from the heart on a bright note pad with black ink.

Susanna with her mother, Clara Marie Reid Shutz

This, too, turns my thoughts to my mom's gifts to me of her time and skill. Those gifts were at work in me like a thread that first got its start in her own mother's heart, to be spun like lace from one heart through to the next in the years to come. And then that thread was spun in my heart.

Thoughts of my mother's heart gifts come to me when I am deep into some new plan of my own, a thing to make or do for some friend or kin. When such an idea comes to mind, then I must be quick to write it down on a note pad so as to not let it slip from my view. Then I will have a fit and firm goal placed in front of me in the days to come. Once I start the plan of what to make, I keep up with the art to its end.

While I wrap this best gift for my child or my friend, I am lost in thoughts of them. I think of how they might use the gift or of what their faces will look like when they spy the gift out of the box or bag for the first time. These thoughts, in turn, lead me to pray for the Lord of Lords to cover my child or friend in His peace and love.

But, at times the gift I've made that stirs me the most is for one who is not as close to my heart as he or she once was. With each fold of the paper and with each twist of the bow as I wrap this gift, I am more sure that God will mend our two hearts and bring strength back to the bond I once had with that friend or kin. When God tells us to give — both to friend and foe — He shows us the way to bring love and peace to our world.

Susanna Shutz Robar

17

All Now Brought Near

Now, thanks to Christ Jesus, you who once were so far away have been brought near by the blood of Christ.

Ephesians 2:13 CEB

When I was a kid we moved from state to state. Every time our home would change. My school could change month to month. Since I was the new kid, I was the one no one knew. I had no roots, no home, no friends. It was a sad time.

When at last we stayed in one spot for my high-school years, I found friends. I was part of a team. I was in the fold. Yet still it was hard to trust, to know I was part of the whole.

Years passed. I found my place in a church. I felt the love of God in Christ, our Lord, and in the family of Christ. Though none had come to the church from the same place — once drawn in, we were one. We were kin through Christ. I was whole. I am whole. Like Ruth I say, with the church: *Where you go, I will go. Where you stay, I will stay. Your kin, my kin, your God, my God.*

As one who, once out, has now been drawn in to the faith, I want all to be a part of Christ. I hear Paul's words as a chance to bring all to Christ. Those far off — now brought near! But those who draw lines to keep some out are wrong. They are not God. They are not of Christ. If I had my way, I would scratch out lines drawn in the sand. To all, I say, "Come to Christ as you are. Come to love. Let us be kin!"

Frank Ramirez

18
WHEN I NEED TO GET AWAY

When I need to get away, I take the canoe, most often alone but once in a while with a friend. As I push from the bank, cares drift away. I'm at peace in the rhythm of it all. Reach, dip, pull, lift, reach. Over and over again. It doesn't take any thought, and I like that. I can turn off the brain, relax and watch the scene in front of me. Often a fish will splash to spread rings over the water. Gulls dip and swoop, but I scan for birds more rare. Pelicans float in search of safe space on a lake. Eagles soar, just a speck until they dive, wings back, claws out.

Once a friend and I slipped under an eagle at rest on a branch. It watched us, and we joked that we were much too big for his lunch, so we were safe from those hooks. We were even safe the time we saw a bear on the shore. Even so, we were glad that he was there, and we were not.

TROY IN HIS CANOE
PHOTO COURTESY DAN PEACOCK

When the day allows, we'll land on some far beach to rest and heat water for tea. We feel no need to speak, for it is quiet and still. It is holy time.

The call to be on the water is strong and wind does not deter.

Inch by inch and foot by foot I find joy in work which makes the arms ache. I focus my mind on plain things; if I allow stray thoughts, waves will fill the boat. I come home tired, but it is a good tired.

Troy in his canoe with son Ian near Welshtown bridge
photo Courtesy Dan Peacock

The canoe is my rest and haven, a chance to reach out to God and for God to reach out to me. In a pinch, a hike will work, but the water's charm speaks to me of grace. These times are scarce, so I am blessed when they occur — touched by the hand of God.

Troy Dennis

19
To Plant a Seed in West Africa

The tall, black man wore a flat cap on his head. It was white, like the long robe that fell to the dry land under his feet. He was the one who had earned the role to lead over all those in that spot in West Africa. His role was to teach the Koran in parts of his and three other lands. The people sent their young boys to board with him and learn Islam. While we were there, six or eight of them had come to learn from him.

As the head over things holy in that West African patch, he made us an offer. "Please come back tonight so my full family can hear what you have to say." His men and women would hoe crops of nuts and okra and tend the herds of sheep until dark.

We said yes. Our team of six went back to the Range Rover. Tim and Anna — those who were in charge of our time there — took us to our rooms at the K'dou motel a few miles away. Our plan was to meet at dark and drive back to the small vill.

When we first came to K'dou, I was agog to find that the room had a full bath, a wall TV, and even crisp, cool air pumped into my room. Near the spic-and -span pool a tall, thin bird roamed here and there. Each morning as we ate in the open-air café, we could hear the women down on the Gambia River as they had to beat their wash on the rocks.

We were 15 hours from any big city. Why such good rooms? I must thank the French for this. In this area's past, they were there on the hunt for gold or other items to add to the wealth of their own home land. The rooms may have been good, but we couldn't say the same for the roads.

Soon after we ate, Tim and Anna came for us. It was dark as we left the town on a dirt road with holes a foot deep. No glow of light lit the way. Tim said he must be wary not to hit a body, alive or dead, in or on the side of the lane. After a short drive, we came to our turn off and then the area to park. We got out of the SUV with a crude lamp and a torch or two and trod down the path.

"Keep a look out for snakes and scorpions," said Tim. In fact, just that day he had killed one of those dread bugs near his home.

The stars and moon shone in the dark sky and made me think of a night long ago in a land not too far away. These folks tend sheep and daily lead lives much like those who left their fields to check out the holy Child all those years ago.

AUTHOR REBA RHYNE WITH THE SPIRITUAL LEADER

In that small area, the best seats had been saved for us. Many tiny frogs leapt in the glow of the fire. Out in the dark of night, we heard feet on the soil. The holy leader said, "More of my family are on the way. We will share our friendship tea as we wait."

Then he said, "We're all here." *How can he be sure?* I thought. I couldn't see a person outside the glow of the fire — but I could hear them.

We were ready. The aim of our trip to West Africa was to share Jesus Christ with any who would hear. What better scene than this to tell the story of His birth and life — to plant a seed for the Holy Spirit to water?

Reba Rhyne

20
Beauty and the Least

Beauty limped from the hen house. Her gold plumes shone bright in the light as the sun rose. From where I worked in the soil, I watched her bump into a bush. She clucked in shame, preened a bit, then scratched at the grass. Her pride may have been fixed, but still I felt sad that her eyes were now dim. Once "queen of the flock," she seemed lost ever since a young hen had robbed her of her post.

Well, that's the way of the world, I thought, but still I felt glum while I cut some rose buds. While I snipped, I mulled over my life. Like Beauty's, my youth also waned, and with my life-roles now over, I had no idea what my fate would be. So each day I moped. Deep in thought, I felt a prick in my thumb and tried to find the thorn, but my eyes are weak now, too. I didn't want to brood over such things for long, so I vowed, there in the rose bed, to trust God just for that day. I bowed and asked that He would help me fuss less over my old age. On a whim, I asked from my heart, "Dear God, please grant me peace."

Just then, I heard what I thought was a peep. There, at the edge of the yard by the field, was our brown hen that had been gone for days. She flounced with joy into the yard, fourteen chicks in tow! Things were quite abuzz for a bit as the hen and her chicks breezed through the open gate into the hen yard. At once, the proud chicks' mom began to strut and peck corn while the chicks ran about. Like me, all the other hens stood and stared, drawn to that sight.

I heard a deep cluck. Faint at first. Then once more. No, not a cluck at all, a call. Rapt, I looked on as Beauty inched over to the chicks and called them again — a scene she had played over time with her own broods. With glee, the small chicks ran near, and scratched and pecked along side each other.

Screech! I looked up and felt a chill. A Red-Tailed hawk swooped above; he would love to feast upon those new chicks. What a fat snack for him! Then God spoke, but not in words.

Beauty and friend

I heard Beauty call once again. In awe, I watched as the wee chicks ran straight to her and under those open wings. Just like that, the chicks were out of the hawk's view. Beauty and each small charge stayed there — firm and still and safe — under the fruit tree by the hen house.

Moved, I stood and mused as my mind flashed back to Psalm 91:4 (NIV):

> *He will cover you with his feathers,*
> *and under his wings you will find refuge;*
> *his faithfulness will be your shield and rampart.*

After a time, I strode back into the house with a warmed heart, a smile, and a soul full of peace. If God had given Beauty her gift of fourteen — the least of the flock — wouldn't He look after me as well? *Yes. Thank you, God. Thank you.*

Patricia Huey

21
SANTA IN THE KUSH

A few years back, while I was stuck high in the Hindu Kush, my job as FOB Chaplain was to cheer up the troops. Once when I made my week's walk-about, I met a non-army American — a right ripe old man, full of joy, plump, and with a full white beard. I asked him if he could get a Santa Claus suit in time for Christmas. He told me that one was even then en route. Then I had my plan.

I sent word to my "care team" of women in Oregon who could find me what I might need — every time. Treats and small gifts were soon en route as well. On the first light of Christmas morn, I grabbed my phone for pics and a bag o' snacks; and then we were off.

All those from the USA beamed with joy and made for Santa. We gave out gifts. All day, we took a lot of pics. The only time we didn't was for a short stop to dodge some straight fire from the enemy. All this time with Santa what shocked me the most were the Afghans. From out-of-view spots, each of them sat low on his loins in a squat.

As one, we Americans began to move about to find the Afghans. With full HUGE grins we strode to them when we saw them. In my poor Pashto, I gave them a grand "khe chare" and then said "za da North Pole yem" to tell them where St Nick came from. Then I waved for them to come to me and meet him.

Then they stood and with great care made their way to us. This was the case through the whole day. Toward eve, I came to those who ran our wood shop and took such care of me and my small church. Even though a photo is not *Shariah*, the Afghans didn't show much more than a quick pause and glance at each other and then all chose to agree to take a "Pic with St Nick."

They squeezed in with Santa and me while my sub snapped a photo of them with new treats in their hands. I raised my arm to show them that photo, and they once more squeezed in close to look. What came next, I'll ever store close to my heart.

As they stared at this odd photo of all of them with Santa, each gave in to a full-gut grin and belly laugh. The joint roar made a sound filled with a joy that I'd not heard in years. I could not help but join them. These closed and strange souls let down their guard so much that at first I was scared, but my fright soon joined their grand laughs and grins, when I saw that they seemed to like all of this very much.

SANTA, JACK, AND THE AFGHAN SOLDIERS

Then the deep truth hit me:

At heart we are the same.

Most of us want Joy in the World.

Most of us want Peace on Earth.

Most of us want Good Will to all.

Then it was plain to see that the path for us to all get what we want can start with me or it could start with thee.

Jack Scott Stanley

22
WHY I LOVE BIG PAPA

Big Papa knows I'm not an easy child.
Since I was young I have not been easy,
And as an adult not much has changed

I have a hard time being still.
I run from Him.
I try to hide.
I'm messy.
I turn away when He's talking
(and even roll my eyes).
I'm a rebel.
I say words that aren't nice —
To Him and to other kids I share this world with.
I can choose the wrong path;
I can choose the wrong friends;
He gives me things and funds that I don't treat well
Or share well.

And yet He loves me.

Even when I run from the saints, He keeps in step with me.

Even when the words have run out,
and all I have left are tears and groans and screams and fists,
He knows what I've said
And He's just glad I came to talk.

Even when I have zero left in me
And I am in that dark pit where my mind can throw me —
Where the lion waits with his amber eyes upon me
And those jaws want to crush me and eat me alive —

Well, Big Papa comes right down into that pit,
Where I am dirty, scared, and weak
And He is big and strong and brave
For the both of us.
When Big Papa comes, He brings the light so I can see again
See that I still have a part of me that can be saved.
The lion won't eat today.

Michelle Ruschman

23
DIARY 1965

What does a sixty-four-year-old woman see when she reads the diary of a twelve-year-old girl? Well, this sixty-four-year-old woman sees the child that she was over fifty years ago.

She sees the first entry on New Year's Day: "Went to Candy's house today. She got a new pony. I rode in a pony cart for the first time." What I didn't know was that it would also be my last time to ride in a pony cart. Did I think my life would be filled with pony-cart rides from then on?

In March, that young girl wrote that Mama said to Billy, "I worry about you being at that march. I wish you hadn't joined the Alabama guard last year, son." The march came to Montgomery, my home town. The folks from the march camped so close to my house I could hear Peter, Paul, and Mary sing that night from my back door. Billy did his job and came home safe; and for the first time, I saw my small world meet the big world.

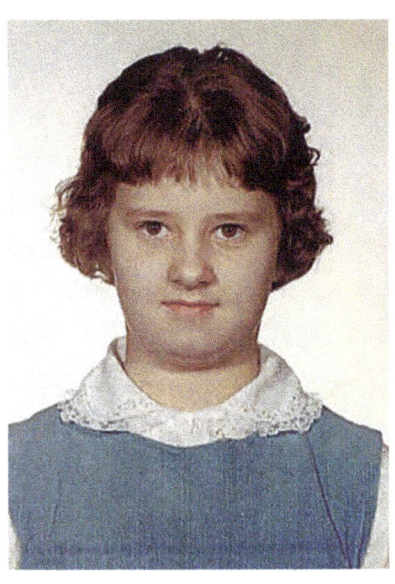

DOTTIE ROGERS AT AGE 12

The girl wrote about school a lot, since that took up so much of her time. She was in the sixth grade. Mrs. King, fresh out of school her own self, loved to learn and helped us love to learn. She taught math and the other usual stuff but also shared her love of art, drama, and show tunes. For one thing, the class learned songs from "South Pacific," since Mrs. King had been in the play.

Mrs. King showed the class that same great ocean on the map. She then showed a place in Asia south of China and said, "Keep your eye on this area. It will be a hot spot." We didn't know what she meant. How did she know that it would be in the news every day for the next few years? I had no idea how much one day it would touch my life when my cousin was killed there.

The twelve-year-old went to church — when her Mom and Dad made her go. She also went to look for God. As time went by, she began to write about the fun she had as part of the youth group. She looked for God and found good friends. She found folks who loved her at church as well as at home. They showed her the God who loved her.

The year 1965 began with my first and only pony-cart ride. It was also my first, though not my only, diary. That, in turn, came to be my first plunge into the joy of using words to give voice to my soul. For over fifty years, I have kept a log in one form or other. I don't write every day, but many of my days are on paper — what I think, what I feel, what I pray, and what I hope for. That twelve-year-old girl is still the inner child of this sixty-four-year-old woman.

Dottie Lovelady Rogers

24
FRENZY TO FANCY

Tick tock — the clock with no mercy.
Rush, rush, push, pull,
Out of my head,
Panic and fear,
Up and down, back and forth,
Too fast to stop.
Can not slow down,
Pull my hair out.
All a blur of moods
Ups and downs, ins and outs,
Push and pull, back and forth.
Bogged down by the world.
What do I do?
Every thing, I see.
All of it!
My world spins round and round,
Mind races and heart pounds.
To get out is all I want!
So I shut my eyes tight.

Then I see him.

He came to me as in a dream.
With mane aflow and eyes so soft.

"Come down — mount."
Eyes shut off from all else,
I still knew what to do.
He has come with peace in his eyes.
I grasped his mane.
We are a go!

Arise with the wind.
'ere I knew it, flight!
My woes and fears lost,
Clock slowed; pain ebbed.
To never stop — I would float with him,
As dreams flood my mind.

The feel of it —
The wind, the only whip, through my hair.
And the soft mane under my thumb.

Again the world below with its needs comes to mind.
My fears and worries too close,
But his eyes —
And my need to be free!
It was as if he spoke.
 "I will be here again, if you need me."
The horse of my fancy!

Sharon Atwood

FICTION

25

Dirge for a Pipe Organ

There it sits, pressed to the back wall of the church and pushed away as if no one cares. *You served us well, but we have no need of you now,* are the harsh but must words. How sad. The wood-cased pipe organ has not been touched in years — not its three tiers of keys, or its white and black stops, or its shiny knobs and full-foot case. The scroll cover has at least an inch of dust on it along with some sheets of music left on the lid — of a song that the choir hasn't sung in years. The church had hoped to sell the organ, but no one ever stepped up to buy it. And so it sits. I think the keys to turn it on must be lost. At one time, the church news sign by the front door said that the staff was in search of them.

The ranks of pipes for the organ still stand tall above the choir loft. Since they've been there so long, they seem as if they are fused into the wall. But the pipes look old; their gleam is worn and dulled through lack of use and lack of care. No more do their sounds pierce the air with bright flutes, soft strings, and reeds that click. No more do their sounds cause the floor and the pews to shake from low bass notes.

I miss the chords and swells that once pealed in such a grand way from that organ. Aunt Mae played with such grace, as her hands and feet would glide along the keys to lead us in hymns and songs. At times her notes brought tears to my eyes and prayers to my lips. The cross often came to mind as she played and pricked the depths of my heart with a sense of love and woe. Most of the time, though, the organ brought joy, hope, and peace. Like Job, I, too, could *"rejoice at the sound of the organ"* (Job 21:12 KJV). But those days are gone now. After

Aunt Mae died, no one could be found to perch on the worn oak bench of the organ. Not one soul. How sad. But then, most in the church don't seem to mind now that we have strings to strum, a bass to pluck, and drums to beat.

Karen O. Allen

26
HOPE

I awoke to a warm January day on an east-coast beach, and for me, all was right with the world. That changed in the blink of an eye when my young son, Ben, fell 25-feet from a deck onto a brick patio. Through CPR, Ben's heart pulsed again, but he did not wake or move. His neck was braced. One lung failed, and he could not breathe on his own. Tubes and wires served to keep him alive. His skull was webbed with cracks. The words "Traumatic Brain Injury" hung in the air. We did not know the state of his mind or if he would live through the night. My heart ached as my joy turned to fear and my fear to grief — all in one fell swoop.

My life had turned dark and full of angst, and for the first time, I faced a world that felt too harsh to bear. Fear and doubt had stepped in as my foes and plagued my heart and mind. So much we did not know: Would our son ever wake up again? What would his life — or ours — be like? I was scared and, even more so, sad. I could not find the words to pray other than, "God, please help us."

Then I read from God's word: *the Spirit intercedes for God's people* (Romans 8:27 NIV). Those words helped me to know that God was there to fight for my son and me. Though I did not know how

KAREN HOLDING BEN IN THE HOSPITAL THREE DAYS AFTER HIS ACCIDENT. HE HAD NOT YET REGAINED CONSCIOUSNESS.

things would turn out at the time, God put my foes of fear and doubt to death, and peace came in to fill my heart.

Once again, hope came to dwell in my heart. That hope was from God — hope for my son's health or at least strength to face the days to come though they might not hold what I had dreamed for him. *We have...hope as an anchor for the soul, firm and secure* (Hebrews 6:19 NIV).

I took heed of those words, and now owe my son's life to them. Some think that Ben's health was in the luck of the draw, but I know it to be the gift of God. So much fell into place for us through it all. Though much went wrong, so much more went right. Ben can breathe on his own again. A rehab team helped him build his strength, walk again, do daily tasks, and speak as he once did. After a month, he was able to come home.

With a touch of His hand, God gave life back to our son. Today, Ben can do all the things his eight-year-old peers can do: run, play, climb, walk, and talk. At times, he will pause to think of how to say what he wants to say, and he is not quite as quick to learn new things; but he does learn. He is blind in his left eye, but he has a good eye and a good life.

About a month after the accident Ben got to go with his family outside the in-patient rehab to make a snowman. Top Left to right is daughter Hannah, Karen, and Kenny (Ben's father) on the bottom left to right is Ben's brother, Jackson, Ben, and Ben's sister, Jenna. Not pictured is Ben's other sister, Lauren, who had returned to college.

My mind often goes back to that day at the beach, and I'm filled with awe at the thought of how far we have come since then. God has blessed us so much.

One might ask why things went our way while for some they do not. I have asked the same. Why? I don't know. What I do know is that God holds our days in His hands; and I praise and thank Him for it all.

Karen Woodard

A year after the accident – l to r: Lauren, Jenna, Hannah, Karen, Ben, Jackson, and dad Kenny Woodard

27
THE BEST PLACE ON EARTH

I lived in California most of my life and thought it was the best place on earth. My husband, Jim, and I had a home on a hill with great views. But we had too much land; our tax bill was too high, and it was hard to keep the land trimmed. So, we sold the house and bought a small home in an RV park in the Phoenix valley and moved in April. We loved it, but then June came with its Arizona heat. It was too hot; we had to find a cool place for a few months.

We tried a few towns, but they were not as cool as we liked. Then, on a trip back home from Colorado, we saw Highway 60 on the map. It went from Interstate 85 in New Mexico to our home in Arizona. As we traced the route, we saw that it passed through Show Low, Arizona.

"Jim, that's the town where my uncle lived," I said. "Remember? Twenty years ago, when we went to see *your* uncle in New Mexico, we took a back road off Interstate 40 and stopped to see *my* uncle in Show Low. He lived near some golf course. I thought it was a weird name for a town."

"You're right. Let's check it out."

The road was full of

FAWN IN THE RIM

turns and hills. A flat tire slowed us down, but we rolled into Show Low on July 4th, just in time to see the bands march and the floats roll down the main street — a small town show.

A drive through town proved that Show Low was just what we liked. At 6400 feet, it is cool and full of pine trees. We felt so at home. The next day we bought the place that would be our home from May to September — only half a mile from where my uncle lived all those years. He, too, came to Show Low for the cool air.

For me were sights to see, back roads to drive, trails to hike, quilt and thrift stores to shop. For Jim were Home Depot, a place to check out books, friends to spend time with, and a church in which to serve. Add to that warm days, cool nights, fields of blooms each month, clouds that float and fluff, skies that do not end, a sun that sets at close of day in a mix of hues and tones, storms that roll through town to cool us, and an arc from God in the sky at the end of those storms. It is a place of awe.

Sunset over Becker Lake

And that name? Two men played cards one day. The one who "showed low" won the deed to the town. True? Who knows? But they named the main drag The Deuce of Clubs, so it must be.

Jim died two years ago, but I still go up the hill each May. This will be my twelfth year to say, "Show Low is the best place on earth."

Sharon Cook

FICTIONALIZED NON-FICTION

28

SOLES

In the arid heart of Mexico, Daisy watched her church's crew who built homes for the poor. Under the hot sun, they ate their lunch and drank cold water; some even poured it over their heads.

Daisy moved into the shade of a bent tree. Under it lay piles of trash, large twigs, and sticks. She spied a dirty shoe on its side in the sandy dirt and tufts of weeds. A dust cloud blew past Daisy. The sole of the shoe seemed to inch away from her and out of view under the sticks.

Did that shoe move? She blinked hard and snuck after the shoe. *There...* Daisy's feet crunched in the dirt as the shoe slid again. *Is that a man's foot?*

Heaps of trash hid a tiny shack made of scrap wood. Its roof was a torn sheet. Ropes tied the hut to the dry, slumped tree next to her. Daisy poked her head into the shack and caught her breath.

A white-haired man sat and stared wide-eyed at Daisy. Soles of old shoes were tied to each of his feet with string.

"What's your name?" Daisy asked in Spanish. "Do you live here?"

"Juan." He said he had lost his job long ago. His adult son lived next door with five kids, but his wife had left them all due to drug use. "I look...um, men make...home..." Juan waved at the crew.

Elena, Daisy's friend, joined them. "I heard you talk —" Elena scanned the shack; her mouth gaped open as she gripped Daisy's arm. "Daisy, this man lives here?"

In low tones, the two girls spoke about what to do. They found Beck, the head of the crew, and told him about Juan.

Beck wiped his face with his shirt. "*Wow.* You mean he's watched us build homes here and never asked for one?"

"Juan told me he's prayed for twenty-five years for a roof. He thought since God was near him with our church group, that maybe his turn was next."

Beck shook his head. "And he just hid back there with his hope and watched us."

"What can be done?" Daisy asked as she glanced at Elena.

"I don't know." Beck frowned. "It's our final day. We've used up most of our wood and nails. I'll see what I can do."

Daisy asked to meet Juan's son.

Six faces peered through the door frame. A few were shy. Juan led Daisy and Elena in to view one small room and no floor.

After Beck peeked through the door, he made some calls on his cell phone. Later, he shared with Daisy and Elena, "All five crews agreed to build Juan's home. They'll haul over any extra items to use. It'll work out well."

After two days, Juan, his son, and kids moved into a four-room, one-bath home with water, a fan, and a floor. At last, he had a roof over his head! Juan stood in his new home with tears in his eyes, "You made…for us?"

Daisy hugged him. "You're right, God was near, and you got more than a roof."

"He saw you and heard you." Beck grinned, "It was your turn, buddy."

E. V. Sparrow

29
In the Beginning

For seven days star dust

flecked His sight

until their heart beats thrummed from

the dust.

"The world," He sighed and

smiled,

    "is very

        very

            good."

                - Creator

Karis Waller

30
BREAD

We rise to life twice.

We start young
as He kneads the soft, slow pulse of our souls
into light loaves of love.

Then He molds us,
pounds us,
knocks us down to the cold hard glass of the bowl
as wind thrusts out of our lungs,
only to rise again, our lives as bread.

We are coaxed by His hand
to bask in the Son that breathes fire,
yet we taste no ash.

We rise as a life to be shared.

So take and eat.
Share in His joy.
Taste and see that
the Baker is good.

Karis Waller

31

THE STACK OF BOOKS

I could not trust what my eyes saw in front of me when I stacked them up in a neat pile. I cringed to get a view of just how out of hand things seemed. Nine books? Not the usual two or three, but nine? How could I read this many books at once? This did not count the Bible and my study books that I do every day.

I just can't seem to read only one book at a time. I grow bored and pick up one more book, and yes, I do read them all. I flit back and forth among them until all books are read, but as a rule of thumb, it's two or three books at a time. Seeing this pile of nine lets me know that I have let this go awry. How had it come to this?

I have fought to keep my mind still, to focus, but this war is far from won. As I age, my mind seems to want more and more. The tales that are told in a blow-by-blow sort of way leave me bored. Being bored, in turn, steers my mind to the next story or the one after. Soon, I have a total of nine or ten books. Who knows how high the count could reach?

I wake today, sick with a flu of some kind, so I vote that this is a great day to curl up and read. I will make a dent in this pile. I climb onto the sofa, nest down in a warm cover, and begin the task. I start with the books where I am close to the end, my plan to make a quick wrap up. Book one, done! Book two, near to being done.

Soon my fever starts to rise. My eyes water, and the words of the book make my head spin. I lay the book in my lap to close my eyes in sleep. Though I am hot, my body feels chilled to the bone. I pull the cover over my head and drift off. My eerie dreams begin to swirl and bob in and out from one tale to the next. I dream the dream of the sick, and see the weird colors, sounds, and light to amuse in a strange sort of way. I hear the line, "It is a tale told by an idiot, full of sound and fury." I am not bored in the least, so I ride the wave of the story in my head. The stack of books will have to wait for some other day.

Adora (Jenny) Calvert

32
My Child Has a Child

My child has a child. Ever since he was born, I often call my daughter and ask if she would mind if I stop by. I know she thinks I'm there only to see her son. But many times, I'm there to watch her watch him.

DAUGHTER HANNAH HOLDING MICHAH

They look at each other in a way that I had never seen in her eyes until then. If they could speak, they would shout *love*. For his part, even as I hold him and tell him a story, he looks for her.

Though still a baby, this sweet boy with his mom's blue eyes owns a stack of books. His mother set it up like this since it was how she was raised. Our clan has always loved books. I began to read to my kids when they were not yet born.

If I could write just one book for her new son, it would speak of God's love, with page after page of blue sky, green grass, and birds that sing, "God made me!" The words would paint a scene of The One who knew this boy before he was born. God placed him in the arms of a father and mother who want what's best for him. They will teach him to love God and choose the right.

As I watch her watch her child, I can't help but think: *One day, sooner than she knows, she'll see her son, with those blue eyes that shout* love, *pick up a book and read of God's plan for our good.*

For today, I will stop and hold my girl long-grown and say, "Sweet, child of mine, spend hours with your boy and books. For one day, too soon, you will wake to find that he is grown with a wife and child of his own."

My child has a child. Thank you, God, for Your grace that knows no end.

Shelley Pierce

33
THE HEART OF GOD

What is in the heart of God?
 Can we ask?
Can we know? Can we go?

If one goes, all should go. One may not make it there, but we'll see if as a group we can — who knows?

As we walk to the heart of God, we have time to talk and come to know each other. We talk about life, hopes, dreams, faith, friends, family, and love.

We talk about what makes us laugh, what feels hard, what is weird, what makes us think, what makes us mad, what makes us sad, and what gives us awe.

We talk about our hopes: the things we can't see yet are right in front of us, the things that make us float — or at least light on our feet — the things that turn into lights when things get dark.

We talk about our dreams and who we want to be. At one time or another, each of us was asked, "What do you want more: to reach the stars and hear the claps of many hands or to learn how to love and be loved?" The choice was ours on our way to the heart of God.

We talk about how we know what is true though we can't see it. We agree, and then at times we do not agree. But we stay on our path to the heart of God.

We talk about a friend who was there for us, when some were not. On good days, we lived, cried, laughed, and played. On bad days, this friend said, "You can do this. I know you can. And if you think you can't, I will still be here."

We talk about our parents, the ones who know and care for us in a way no one else does. When we were small and even now that we are big; they are the ones who hold us, hear us, teach us, let us know that we are known. They are the ones who will not let us go.

Each of us has talked and come to know each other one of us as we draw near to the heart of God. We talk about love, those who live in the depth of us and — if love is true — we in them. They may be family, or friends, a church brother or sister who draws close to our souls. They are why we live and move this day, on, and on.

Now, we are here. God will not let us see, but if we want to know, God does not mind. All we do is ask.

What's in God's heart?

It's you.

Adam Benson

34
WORLD REACH

Jesus tells us to *"go and make disciples of all nations"* (Matthew 28:19 NIV). While I want to obey, I do not want to live in a hut in Africa, and I can't speak Spanish. But I have found a way to reach the world where I do not have to move.

True, I do have to drive two miles to a church; once there, each Tuesday night I can talk to folks from all over the world. I teach English to those who do not speak it — or at least not well. They were born in Asia, South America, Central America, and Europe, but they now call the U.S. home.

The goal is for my class not only to learn English but also to learn about God and His love for them. I use a Bible verse each week to help those in my class learn new words. I also

LEFT TO RIGHT: NULEK JENNINGS, NOEMI RUIZ, PONG REIDY, WRITER ALICE MURRAY, AND BEATRICE HARRACH

show God's love through how I act with each pupil in the class. Just being there says much; they know I work all day and then come to teach them at night for no pay.

Due to my ESL class, I know that when Jesus says "Go," it may not mean I have to leave the United States. I can reach those from a far away land right in my local area. It is a small world after all, and all of the world needs God's love — even those close at hand.

Alice H. Murray

35
A Gentle Answer

The young man sighed as he rang up my items. When he reached for the white peach in the clear bag, he rolled his light blue eyes.

"Oh great." He sighed again. "What is this?" His tone was harsh, as if I had tried to steal the fruit and he'd caught me.

"A white peach," I said.

He pressed his lips into a firm line, punched a code, and reached for the next bag.

He must have had a long day, I thought. I had to think of a way to feel for him. If not, I would end up using a harsh tone of my own.

Once he rang up my last item, I keyed in my store code. "That failed, ma'am." Again, his tone was sharp, like the knives sold in aisle five.

My pulse boiled. Mean words rose to my tongue, but I tried once more to stop them. I thought of Proverbs 15:1: *A gentle answer turns away wrath but a harsh word stirs up anger* (NIV),

Help me not to speak harsh words, I prayed.

"Let me try again," I said as I keyed the code once more.

"Won't work." His stare was as cold as ice. "I guess I'll find the store card to use for you."

His boss should know about this, I thought as I stood there. But the Spirit nudged me and said no.

What should I do, Lord?

Then it hit me: My niece is a lot like the young man in front of me. Due to her past, her mood goes up and down. It's hard for her to stay kind and calm all day long.

Life may be just as hard for this clerk. What if he hurts in his mind or soul in ways I can't see?

With my own strength, I would have fussed and sighed right back at him. But that only would have made him feel worse. I just prayed for the young man to learn with time and have a good week.

When he came back and keyed the code, I paid for my items. "Thanks for your help on that," I laughed. A grin came to his face.

As I walked away with my bags, I told him, "Thank you" with a kind smile. And as I walked out of the store, I gave God my thanks.

Lauren Craft

36
LOVE AT FIRST SIGHT

"Get up. I found it." It was Christmas Eve, and my wife, Rosemary, was sure about what she would give me.

"Good. Go get it. See you when you get back."

"No, no. You have to drive. It's clear on the other side of town."

"Give the store your card," I said. "They can hold it."

"They don't take credit cards."

"What? I want to sleep. Ask if they have one at a store on the west side."

"There's only the one store," she said. "And don't ask. This is the last one. They will hold it till we get there."

I threw off the covers. "Fine."

"This will be the best gift of your life."

With no one on the road, we made short work of the trip. "Pull up at Target," said my wife.

If it's in there, I could have slept. I thought.

"Get out," Rosemary said.

"Why? I'll wait in the truck. Go get it. I'll keep my eyes closed."

"It's not here."

If not, then where is it?

"You can't go with me. If you, do you'll know as soon as I park."

"I told you I would keep my eyes closed."

"Open the door," she said.

I got out.

"Go in and wait. I'll get you when I come back."

Rosemary found me. "I have to get one more thing," she said. "Wait here."

I sat down. "Just hide it."

"It won't fit in the cab."

"Put it in the bed," I said.

"I can't. 'too much wind. I'll be right back." She left.

"Come with me. Close your eyes. Keep them closed." I did as I was told. We walked hand in hand. "Don't peek." I had no idea what I'd see. "Open your eyes."

It was love at first sight — for both of us. In the back of the other truck, I saw a face with a shiny wet nose and two big brown eyes. A long tongue tried to lick my face. The large red bow sat on her head. I hugged my dream.

I'd wished for a Golden Retriever but didn't think that one day I'd own one. As I hugged Bear, she rested her head next to my face. Tears of joy rolled down my cheeks. In the years to come, she moved with us to Nevada, then California, and back to Arizona.

On her last night, we slept in the same bed. But she didn't leave me. She still lives in my heart.

Jeff Adams

37
THE LAST VERSE

The story began about ten years prior to the end. Mom had just passed away, which left a big hole in Dad's heart. At least we knew that we would never again have to go through the loss of a parent to Alzheimer's. At times, Dad's mind seemed a bit foggy, but whose mind wouldn't — with all the stress of Alzheimer's?

Later Dad began to court a widow we knew from church, and they both found a new spark in life. Soon they let us know they planned to tie the knot, and they did. But while the stress of Mom's Alzheimer's was in the past, Dad's mind and his use of words grew worse. We had to face the fact that he had some form of dementia.

LESTER STERKSON
WITH HIS HYMNBOOK AND BIBLE

My stepmother asked that Dad stay at our home while she went on a trip out of town to visit one of her daughters. This was the first time he stayed with us, but later the health of both Dad and my stepmom began to fail. Our house became his home. Over the next years, my father began to lose more and more of his life. After about three years, we had to begin to feed him. One day, when Dad had been with us for about four years, we had to call 9-1-1 once again. This time we brought him home with no hope to live. For twelve days he lay there — not able to eat, drink, talk, or move. It was so much like Mom's death.

Through it all, I thank God that Dad never lost his sweet frame of mind. He was a man of strong faith, whose life had been very much tied to the church. Not being able to go to church was hard. But we kept alive the hymns and songs of the church. We would often watch a film of a group of saints who would use their gifts to sing great hymns and songs and would put their whole hearts into each song.

One of the last twelve days of Dad's life, a hymn came to my mind over and over. But why? It didn't seem to fit. Since it wouldn't leave my mind, at last I said, "Okay, God, I guess you want me to sing that hymn to Dad." I got out my hymn book and turned to page 391: "'Tis So Sweet to Trust in Jesus." I sat by Dad's side and began to sing in a hushed tone. After the first verse I sang one more, then went on to sing all the way through the last verse:

"I'm so glad I learned to trust Thee,
Precious Jesus, Savior, Friend;
And I know that Thou art with me,
Wilt be with me to the end."

Of course! That was why God had led me to sing it — for the last verse. The thought that God cared so much for Dad warmed my heart and held me up through the slow loss of one more dear parent. Since then, each time I hear that hymn I think of that day and a Father's love.

Joanne Fleck

38

DON'T DRINK THAT – DON'T EAT THIS

"Don't drink that!"
"Don't eat this!"

It's all I hear from my wife, Michelle, these days. I dare not pick up a can of any drink until I've read the pesky label first. Why? Here's why! When she sees me take a drink the first thing she'll ask is:

"Do you know what's in that?!?!"

Then there's no way to reply and keep the peace.

If I say "no", she will take the can and read the food label to me. She'll read every word on that label. Yes, ev-er-y word.

If I say "yes," she'll say: "Tell me what's in it!"

Now I'm pinned in! I'm going down and I know it.

So what to do? Do I even dare read the label aloud? I know that as soon as I start to read the list it won't be long until I have to say the "s" word... You know, "sugar."

Then, with a straight stare in her eyes and brows raised, she'll say: "How much sugar?"

<Sigh.> Why do I do this again and again? Unless I lie or hide what I've done, she gets me every time. Even when I do lie, she isn't swayed. She knows. But how???

This scene plays out the same with drinks and foods alike. There's no way out!

But here's the good part; I've learned some things — like how much extra sugar has been added to foods I never knew had it. Yes, foods like pasta sauce and dried fruit have some kind of sugar in them — even many so-called sugar-free drinks! Sugar adds no good thing and keeps our health less than 100%. The fact is, the over use of sugar has left many a friend or loved one with poor health, bad teeth, and an obese body.

I did not know this until I read the label, but each one of my drink of choice packs 59 grams of sugar; and I tend to drink two in a row. That's 118 grams of sugar in what I drink alone!

"What then shall I drink?" I ask her.

"Drink water." she says, "Just drink water."

As told to Michelle Walker-Wade

39
HOPE DURING A TOUGH YEAR

In January 2001, death came too soon for my uncle. At the same time, we got the news that my husband had the "big C" at the age of forty-seven. Fear came to roost in the months that passed as we got ready to wage war with this foe.

While we still reeled from the scary health news, my mom was told her heart would not last more than a few weeks. I wept. *Why God? I still need her here. She has great grandchildren to get to know and love. I don't think I can take any more.*

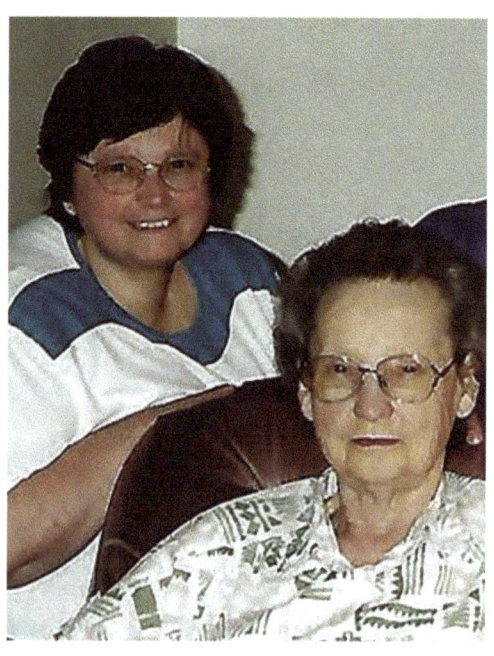

CAROL HARRISON WITH MOTHER, ROSELLA CLARK, JUST AFTER DIAGNOSIS

But in August, the road wound down to a pit so deep with a late-night call no one wants to get. My father-in-law was dead. "How can this be?" we asked. He had crops in the field and cows and pigs to care for. Who would do the work? My husband could not be in two sites at once and had to go each day to try to fight his health foe.

Three more months later, we laid my mom to rest. Tears and more tears. Fear that hope had left for good. I knew God had kept her here for more time than we had thought, but it still felt too soon for her to leave us.

Grief clung to me like a too-tight shirt that left no room to move — or even breathe. *Where are you, God? Do you feel the pain of my loss in this year as I drown, weighed down with no rest in sight? Do you hear my cry and see my tears?*

I look back and see small stabs of light in the dark times that year. I ended up being able to spend months with mom and hear her tell tales of her youth. Some folks sent a meal or gave a hand with tasks that had to be done. Friends lent their ear and gave hugs. With words that brought a smile to my face, they let me know they were there for me. The long-stemmed, dark blood-red rose a clerk gave me didn't die for two weeks or more. Little things like these let me see hope even in life's tough times.

I also found hope in my Bible with these words in Psalm 34:

I sought the Lord and he answered me and delivered me from all my fears....The eyes of the Lord are on the righteous and his ears are attentive to their cry....The Lord is close to the broken hearted and saves those who are crushed in spirit. (vv 4, 15 and 18, NIV).

These words felt as if they were penned just for me. *God, you heard my cry and caught my tears. You knew my fears. Help me trust in you as I climb the steep hill out of one tough year.* I still miss my mom. The cows, pigs and crops have been dealt with. My husband won his fight with the big C, but life was not the same. I was not the same, but I did see stabs of light that God used to show me hope even in the next tough times that would come.

Carol Harrison

FICTIONALIZED NON-FICTION

40

Sister

"Load up." Lucy said as she tried to keep the tears out of her voice. "Come on, Sunny."

Sunny's eyes were soft and brown. He let out a whine.

"Be a good boy. Load up."

Sunny sprung into Lucy's old SUV and sat in his spot.

In the back, she had his dog crate, a few toys, and a third of a bag of dog food. It was the kind he didn't like, but all she had left.

She laid her hand on the soft scruff of fur under his white-and-gold chin.

"Please, Jesus," she said under her breath, a plea she had said each day since she took ill.

One doc had said the C word. One doc thought his knife would fix it, but he didn't know what IT was. She was tired of doing this alone.

"Please, Jesus," she said again, never able to come up with the right words for the deep need she felt.

She took the exit off route 67 by the strip mall where the pet store was. She began to look for a lady in a blue truck.

Lucy turned to her dog. "You'll have a good life. I'm too sick to keep you these days," she told him. Her tears fell fast and hard. Sunny had come to her when he was eight weeks old, and now he was ten years old. He was all she had left. "It's for your good, Sunny. Jesus, let this be the right thing. Let her be kind."

A girl in a pink shirt with long black hair got out of the truck. "You must be Lucy, and this must be Sunny," she said. "I'm Maya." Her voice was sweet, and she had kind eyes.

"I've read your texts. We should talk. I pray for you and have ever since I first saw your ad about Sunny. I know you want what is best for him, but if I may be so bold — I don't think this is what's best for you. I could feel your pain in each word of the ad and in your texts. He's your friend. He gives you peace when your days are long."

"But, I —"

"Please hear me out," said Maya. "From your texts, I feel we have many traits alike, and I think we could be fast friends, so this is how I'd like this to go — on a trial basis, of course. But I think you need Sunny. And Lucy, I think you need me. I live close by here and have time in the day to come take care of Sunny and help you where I can. It makes sense to me that you stay with the pup you love. Then, if things change, I will take care of Sunny, so you will know he's safe."

"No Maya, you are young. You don't need to take care of me. Who am I to you?"

"You're my sister in Christ, and I will help, for I know we have met for more than Sunny's sake. Let me be your friend. It's time you got help."

Leah Hinton

41

To Lyndell with Love

Dear Lyndell,
  Your mom said you asked how I got to be a pastor. A wise man once said, "God calls you to the place where your deep joy and the world's great thirst meet." I hope you read this not as a strict rule but as a tale of love.

I was born in Nineveh, a small town in Indiana. Life was hard. My mom sought ease through pills. My dad was lost in his work. Their friends put beer in my cup and laughed as I fell to the floor.

The school album shows me at age three, in a crowd at a game. My eyes fixed on the action, filled with glee for the globe of a ball.

I had a drive to be the best in high school – in sports and in class. I went out with a girl. Our first date had to be to church. She sought more than a kiss or a touch. I craved more than her faith had to offer.

College was a place I mixed songs with sex, thoughts with drugs. The God I had come to know went up in smoke. In place of the Word were words that sought truths to sink the Truth. Rights to ruin us; no rules to live by.

I wrote a book called *Life (in obvious places)*. At the end, a flirt named Claudia Matson asks, "Why don't you write a love story?"
"I don't know any," I say.

I took a job at a mill and was led to a small church in the woods, filled with folks who made room for me in my stained clothes that smelled of smoke. One day, on my way to church, I saw a woman in a torn coat in a bank lot. She looked out of place. I pulled off and tried to help. She didn't know where she was. I didn't know where she lived. We were both lost.

I drove her to a church where all were dressed in their Easter best. An usher gave her tea and a treat. He sat with her and helped her find her way home. I left that church in tears. I had found strength to be weak in a place of grace.

I went back to school to serve God with my mind, in hopes my body and soul might catch up. In class I learned how not to talk about God. In field work, I found God. In the joy of a boy who would never speak. In the songs of teens who longed to be free. In the tears of a man who prayed next to his wife's death bed.

I say I found God. But it was God who found me. I just didn't run away.

    Love,
        Grandpa

Tony Roberts

42

G G

"Is your dog named 66?"

"No, it's G G."

In my haste to fill out the info sheet for my dog, her name looked like "66."

"G G is short for God's Gift."

"Really?"

Then I told her G G's story.

On a warm, August day in 2004, I was in the woods with a Rhodesian Ridgeback hound named Casey. I walk and pet sit dogs, so five days a week, I would drive Casey to the woods for a mid-day walk. On one of the trails, a young man and woman came toward me. Next to them stood a small, gray dog with no ID tag. The man asked if I knew who owned the dog. I said I didn't.

He told me that the dog had tagged along with them the whole time they were on their hike; then they told me they were going to go.

"What about this dog?" I asked.

"It's not ours."

The man and woman hiked down a path that led out of the woods, and the small, gray dog dashed after them. I ran and picked her up. She barked and squirmed in my arms as the two got in their car and drove off. I held her as she began to pant and seemed in dire need of water. On our way to take Casey home, the lost dog paced and barked in the front seat, while Casey sat mute in the back. At Casey's house, I brought in the small dog and gave her a drink. Then I took her back to my car. While I drove, she whined. At home, I called the dog pound. After the agent got there, I told him where and how I had found the dog. Then he told me what he thought: All along, the man and woman had planned to get rid of their dog in the woods. Then, when they saw me with Casey, they thought I would take the other dog if they said it wasn't theirs.

State law calls for a lost dog be held for ten days. This gives the owners time to call and claim their pet. As the ten days passed, no one ever called for the small, gray dog. She had no micro-chip ID with her name and that of the owner. No lost dog signs showed up in the woods, also no ad in the paper under "Lost Pets."

The small, gray dog was in need of a home. I knew deep in my heart that she was meant for me to have. She was God's gift to me. That is why I named her "G G." In February of 2004, my 14-year-old cairn, Scruffy, had died. As I grieved my loss, my sister Sandi said, "Debbie, someday God is going to bring a dog back into your life." And six months later, on a warm August day, He did.

Debbie Pierce

43
FOR THE SAKE OF CHRIST

Twelve times I've been to India, and each time I've been struck by the hurt and want I've seen there. But never has my heart ached as much as when I met the men from the state of Orissa. Though their huts had been burned to ashes, their crops were gone, and many had died, they still loved Christ so much that they, too, would die for Him. They told of the hate for God. Of how men who were paid to keep folks safe, turned on them and killed them. Some took a whip and beat the man who led their town, and also the one who spoke for God. Then they threw them in the lake and held them down until they were dead. It was too, too sad.

I couldn't stay long in India, for I had to be in Japan to teach those who learned English from a book I wrote. In Japan, I spoke at a church with young folks who came from China to study in Japan. They asked me: "Are there any in the world who walk with Christ who don't live in China or the U.S.?"

"Yes," I said. They asked where.

"In all the world."

They were not sure I spoke the truth. They said, "Tell us of some."

So I told them of the burned huts in Orissa, India, and of the men who were thrashed, then drowned.

"Why did they do it?" the young ones from China asked.

"So that no one else would dare to talk about God," I said. "Many died for Christ's sake."

When they heard that, they fell to the floor to cry and pray. One young man called out, "But they are our brothers and sisters in Christ! I will give all my money to help them."

One by one, each in the room said the same. For most, it was the money that they had saved up to pay for school.

I didn't plan to go back to India soon, so I sent the money to a man I knew there. I told him he should get it to the right place as fast as he could. He said he would take care of it. So I put it out of my mind.

Three years later I went back to India to speak to a large group. I told them of the church in Japan and the young folks from China who sent their school funds to India. Noise came from the back of the room. I paid it no mind — until it grew so loud that no one could hear me speak.

Then two women dressed in white clothes came

THE CHINESE STUDENT IN JAPAN WHO FIRST GAVE HIS UNIVERSITY TUITION

down the aisle with a man who spoke English. He said they were the wives of the men drowned for their faith. Cruel men had locked the wives in the burned church and left them there to starve to death. The next day, when they heard steps by the door, they thought the

THE TWO WIDOWS WITH THE PASTOR WHO CAME FORWARD WITH THEM

evil men had come back to kill them.

But it was not them. Two strange men came in. "We brought you a gift from your Chinese family in Japan," they said.

The women, who had never heard of Japan, were scared. But the men took them to a safe place and gave them the money. "We used it to buy cows and sell the milk," they told us. "With the milk, our young ones grew healthy and strong. We hired other mothers to help us."

The mothers earned so much that others called them rich. But they didn't keep the money. They used it to start a school so that each child could learn to read and write.

"You gave us new life," the two wives said, as they wept and kissed my hands.

The room was still. Then one voice sang out, "Blessed be the name…." One by one, others joined in: "You give and take away. You give and take away. My heart will choose to say, Lord blessed be Your name."

He does give, and He does take away. And then He gives again. Blessed be His name!

THE TWO WIDOWS WITH AUTHOR KAY MARSHALL STROM

Kay Marshall Strom

"Blessed Be Your Name" by Matt Redman

44
SLOW, SURE STEPS

As I hiked to Mission Peak in Fremont, California, thick fog met me. New to that trail, I failed to see how I could find my way.

At the start of the trip, in a school lot, I met with blue sky, lush grass, blooms, and a broad red trail. Now in the pea-soup fog, I could see only a few feet in front of me. My steps were many because my strides had to be short.

My mind cried, *Am I on the right trail? Will I be left with shame and not pride in my climb when I fall off a ledge or ridge? Who will find me if I do? Could I die in the fall?*

JON ON THE TRAIL

Even though I couldn't see one soul, I knew that I was not alone. Some near me kept me from wrong side paths. At last, my small steps up a steep grade led to the top. Yay! But what a trip!

In life, small firm steps and a guide also help when we are in the fog. Once, when I lost my job, I gave up on my life path. With tears, and the Word open, I cried to God. "Lead me! I give up on my own course. It's my fault. I am lost. Where will we go? Where will we live? Why go on?"

But God knew His plan, and the path best for me. He led through the tears and the fog; He led my wife, our kids, and me to a new home and job. This new home — on a ridge — had a great view, lush grass, and the blooms of Spring. God had led, in love, through the fog.

Jon Drury

45
WHY IS HE STILL HERE?

What have I missed?
It's hard. I've prayed, a lot.
I know You can change this, God.
You could take him out of my life.
I can't change him or his heart . . . but You can.
Why haven't you stopped this strife?
Have I prayed the wrong way?
I don't want to pay for this war with my peace.
Will You help me?

How would You have me look at this, God?
What am *I* blind to that You could help me see?
Your Word tells us, when they hurt us, don't turn away.
That's what You did.
You asked us to trust you,
To do things Your way. Not the way we feel.
Why?
You said You see it all, and in the end, You've got our backs.
You said You are just.
Can I trust that?
Can I trust Your way is best?
You tell us to love those who hate us.
Period.
You call us to trust
You with our hurts, to let them go.

All I know —
I don't want this pain any more.
Will you help me,
Help me love this one who strikes out at me?
From the cross, You asked God to set them free,

Those who'd hurt You,
Since they didn't know what they had done.

From You, I know that to hate him is wrong.
I want the same grace You gave them.
I want to be right with You.
As I choose to trust You, to do this Your way,
I feel the load lift.
The hurt that clenched my heart has let me loose.
My joy came back to life.
I have to choose to love him every day,
As You have.
When I do, I keep my peace,
And it's worth it all.

Sharon Fincannon

46

VALID ID

"I need to see your ID, Ma'am." The fact that I have just made a vocal claim to my full name doesn't seem to mean a thing to the clerk. Duty bound, she stares back at me and waits until I show proof — by way of my ID card — that I am whom I claim to be.

Very often when I hear a name — even a name I haven't heard in a long time — right away, my mind's eye clicks on an image. This image may be a face, a place, an event, or just what I have come to think about him or her from my own point of view. Any or all can lead me to a "back story," based on my past with this woman or man. Then, like the clerk who looks at the ID card, I rely on what I "see" about this name, be it good *or* bad.

Proverbs 22:1 (NIV) tells me *a good name is more desirable than great riches; to be esteemed is better than silver or gold.* Wealth (or the lack of it) does not come into play in the "back story" of one with a good name, for a good name can't be bought or sold; it can only be earned — and *kept* — through trust.

I care about what image my name brings to the mind of one who knows me. I hope it leads not just to a "back story" from the past but to a "now story"— proof that I am who I claim to be, that my ID is valid, that my name is duly matched to an image earned — and *kept* — through a trust worth more than gold.

Suzanne D. Nichols

47
Last Act

In a land quick
to say no to
its own thirst,
You were a gush of
Yes —
fresh and clear
a surge from your heart
full of care
to give
Your life
for mine

(while I ask You
about rules
and that tax,
bread and
wine left
to dry on
the table),

but when, in that last act
You burst the bonds,
all the pain
the sin
of this cut-off life
now Yours,
Your soul
leapt clear
of nails
and sword's slash.

You broke
into whole
light
God
again
and
You took me with You.

Marcia Lee Laycock

48

DOWN THE STREET

The black Doberman Pincer places its paws on the glass panes of the door, its eyes wild. It bares its teeth and barks at me. A Toy Terrier hurls its tiny body just below its big brother — a tenor to the deep bass. I was just about to knock on the door and then back away, happy to leave in one piece.

I go door to door for a good cause and have for years. These days, those who open the door don't have the time to talk. Nos are many, but the usual is, "I gave at work." Some of those who live close by look shocked at the thought that they might give up any of their hard-earned cash, even for a good cause.

I pick my way through one more snowy path. My boots have good grips, but I have not thought about the lack of warmth from the sun in the months of ice and snow. I zip up my jacket as far as it will go and rue my choice not to wear any gloves. My idea was to free my hand to write a thank you slip — should the need arise!

The next house is quiet. The door opens at the first knock; light and good smells flow out. I stand on the wide porch and show the ID that hangs from the bright cord on my neck.

"I'll get my wife," says the man who opens then shuts the door.

Cold creeps through my bones. I like the change they've done to the front of their house. The new deck is well made with river-rock posts. The only thing is that the wood makes me slip in the cold.

"Here it is," says the woman. She opens the front door a few feet.

"I'll write you a tax slip," I offer. The woman nods. I stay out on their front deck, by now my hands red and shaky. I stoop over and write on my knee, rip off the page and give it to her. As I take the twenty-dollar bill, the woman closes the door. I go down the steps with care and stuff the cash in my case. This is my last call and the only money given.

Who are these folks who live on the same street as I do? I wonder.

I know who lives right next door and even the ones next to them, but after that are very few I can call *friend* — after twenty-three years in the same house.

The next week brings big snow to the city. My husband and I dig white stuff for three days straight. On the fourth day, the sun shines and big drips slide down the front door into the hall of our home.

Men come to work on the snowy roof. An hour and $325.00 later, a giant mound of dense snow and ice sits on the drive. It takes my husband and me two hours to chop down the pile to half of its glory. Tired, we rest on our spades.

"Need a snow mover?" calls out a man, as he leans over his snow bank.

We look at each other and smile. Good sorts live in this area after all.

"Oh yes," comes our reply.

Sheila Humphrey

FICTIONALIZED NON-FICTION

49

HANNAH'S SON

Hannah held her small son close to feel his soft, slow breath on her face.

He's here. My son is here.

She stilled her thoughts so she could hold all the joy she knew, wrapped in soft cloths, near to her heart. A tear of pure bliss slipped down her cheek. She smiled.

God is good. He is. He's heard my cry. He has not failed to help me.

She thought of all the days and years that she'd feared this day would be lost to her, that she'd go through life with no child born from her womb. It would have been a life she could not bear to live, a fear worse than death — at least to her.

When Elkanah had asked if he was not worth more than ten sons to her, she'd been wild with grief. Ten sons? What kind of man would ask his wife that? Her love for Elkanah could not hide her lost hope that she would bear him a son. How would she know if she could love him more or less than if she had ten sons? What a time she'd had to sort out her heart. She'd ached from the sore, sad, and bad thoughts that had come to mind.

Hannah had prayed with all her heart and soul — but not with words that could be heard by any but God. Then Eli, the priest, had blessed her, and she'd dared to hope that her time would come. And now it had!

The grief was gone. The tears had been hard and real, but they ruled no more. The taunts and jeers of Peninnah had stopped for weeks now. The sad looks from friends had turned into glad smiles as they came to see the child who'd been so long to come to Hannah and Elkanah.

With Samuel so close, so real, so new to this earth, she could rest in the truth of how God had shown His kind ways to her. No one need tell her that God is good. Now she knew it in her own heart.

The child stirred. She kissed the top of his head, the small patch of thick, dark hair so soft on her lips. Soon he would wake and want to feed, but for now he slept.

Sleep on, my son. You are mine. I will not have you in my arms for as long as I might have, had I not vowed to give you to the Lord. You are mine and you are His, as well. When the day comes that I must part with you, my dear son, I will pray that God will use you for His Name's sake. Your life will be great in the Lord, my child. But for now, you rest near my heart. My love for you knows no bounds. My arms once ached to hold you, and one day they will ache when you are gone. But we have this time, right now. Sleep on, my Samuel. Our God has heard my cry.

Carol Schafer

To read about Hannah in the Bible, see 1 Samuel 1–2:21.

50
THE CALL OF THE BEACH

At dawn, it is still — yet not. With few on the beach, wide and clear is the space on the sand. A bird flies by with a squawk or a chirp. From a spot down the beach, a kite makes its way into the sky for as long as the beach rules allow time for it to roam free. The sand is wet and hard from the tide that has come up and gone out; dark stains show the tide's path. Soft warmth feels like a smile from the sun as it holds back on its glare in this first light. Waves wash over my feet as I walk while even more crest just off the shore in their bid to start the day.

I walk to breathe, to cleanse, to rinse off the storms of life that can bring clouds to the heart, mind, and soul. I walk to talk to my God; I walk to see and hear what He has made. At noon, the still has gone. Now I walk to work, to strain and to sweat, as the sun's rays beat down on me in a strong blaze of light and heat. I walk to hear and see life up close. Kids of all ages play in the sand, swim in the sea, surf the waves, sit in the sun, eat a noon meal, stretch out for a nap, read books in a lounge chair, and dip their toes at the water's edge.

As I hike down the shore, my feet sink into soft piles of sand as my toes grip its grains. The waves crash and pound the shore to echo in my ears as I walk; they splash my feet and spray my legs. At dusk, the still peeks its head back in. Now I walk to rest. I walk to think. I walk to just be.

Once more, the space on the beach is wide and clear. The tide comes up to bring the day to an end. Kites soar to the sky. Balls are thrown back and forth. Dogs bound into the ocean. Chairs, once a place to get lost in the pages of a book, are now a place to watch the sun as it sets. Like the dawn, the dusk is still yet not still. And so, I walk. Dawn, noon, and dusk — when I can see for miles, the beach calls me to walk.

Sue Rosenfeld

51
The Ache to Be Whole

In a body scrunched into a ball,
Caught up in her fears,
There hides a tiny girl
Whose face is washed by tears.

He looks in from the outer edge,
And aches to join the crowd.
He feels like he will never be
Known and loved and proud.

Laughed at by the other kids
For how her body looks,
She finds the friends that her heart craves
In the leaves of her books.

He's run away from peril
In his war-torn land;
He's scared to stay and scared to go;
He's scared to take a stand.

Her body has been razed
By years of pain that will not yield,
She's tried to ease the strain,
But has no strength to raise a shield.

Those of every age who ache
Just want to be made whole.
They long for rest to come and fill
Their body and their soul.

When Jesus spreads His loving arms,
His reach will touch us all;
He wraps the very outer fringe
Where those who hurt have sprawled.

He soothes away our tears
And heals every pain.
Our fears will melt away;
His love breaks every chain.

He binds our many wounds with care,
Those veiled and those we see.
Jesus is the only One
Whose touch can make us free.

Liz Kimmel

52

THE BIG DATE

So here it is — the day of the big date. It will be at my place, just the two of us, and I am the cook…for the whole meal…from scratch. To say that I want it to go great is too mild. I want to cause a bang like an 18-wheel truck that just drove over a giant beach ball.

To pick the main dish I make an overt choice not to cook up a meal whose name rhymes. Sad to say, that crosses off Surf 'n Turf, Crunch 'n Munch Soup, and Ideal Eel Stew (which is just wrong to begin with). Shoo Fly Pie also fails to make the cut. I mean, how could I draw near to the table dressed to stun while I exude charm from every pore and say, "This fine night our grand and noble dish is Bean-y Wean-y Hash"?

At last, I choose "Stefanie Blais." This dish works in many ways. For one, when they hear its name they will say, "Huh? What is that?" "Is 'Stefanie Blais' the name of the chef who created it?" "Is it what it's made of?" Having no clue as to what it is also makes it deep and dark — the sphinx of foods, one that seems far from our frail, boring life. It also sounds French. Thus, it stands out among food names. Never mind that it means that I have to stuff a steak with small bits of shrimp and other things that I would in no way ever buy and then wrap the whole thing in puff-pie dough. It is a risk, but my thought is that even if I swing with my eyes closed at a ball thrown at 100 mph I can once in a while hit one out of the park — right?

So I am busy on the main course. I saw those chefs on TV whose hands fly as if they are playing a piano as they chop up the food. Sad to say, my hands move more like bored snails. I cut the shrimp into bits of the exact same 1/16th of an inch wide. An M.D. would have gasped in envy.

I have 72 proofs, 65 of them backed up by the Bible, as to why I should use a store bought Bernaise Sauce in lieu of a bid to make it from scratch, but do I obey what I say? No! *My own sauce will taste so much more fresh and bright,* I think. I did find a way to make a Mock Bernaise Sauce but that idea just seemed to make fun of me.

The hour of the epoch is very near and my opus is still very far from done. My sauce is stuck to the base of the pan, and I will wager my shoes that it will taste like burnt books. The puff-pie dough made a giant puff and then fell back down in a swoon. With a plan that is more folly than savvy, I put the green beans in a pot to steam and top them with my own ghee/herb sauce only to find the sauce doing a breast-stroke in the hot water that lies under the sieve…and the beans.

Then I hear a knock at the door. I do not even have time to leap down the back stairs and get take-out. As she sits down at the table, I place the plate of woe in front of her. I add more chives on the top to draw her eyes away, so she will not see what is below. Once I sit down myself, I have to strain every sinew in my neck to keep my head from an ill-fated fall into the soggy mashed yams. I emit a faint sob.

She cuts off a piece of steak. I smile like a wax head. She puts it into her mouth. I clench my teeth. She speaks. "This is great."

Bob LaForge

53

THIS TIME

On February 14th, I watched the news with tears in my eyes. For the twelfth time in the first six weeks of this year, shots were fired in a school. This time (and how awful that I have to say "this time") it was at Marjory Stoneman Douglas High School in Parkland, Florida. This time, seventeen died, fourteen of them teens. Three adult staff also died as they tried to help or shield the kids they loved and spent time with every day.

My heart aches every time I hear a story like that, but this time the story hits close to home. My niece lives in Lake Worth and works just a few miles from Marjory Stoneman Douglas; she knows folks who lost a child. Her son knows one of the girls who died through their years-long role in the local dance scene; it has been a big part of both their lives. When I asked my niece how they are, she said, "Numb. And also sad." Of course, they are.

Over and over, I ask myself how this can be. A young man (or, if we agree with those who study the brain and say the area of it that guides choice grows until we reach age 25, he is still a boy) has killed many. His prior acts and his anger had caused folks to see him as a threat. How could his cries for help not have been heard? Who had looked away? Have I looked away from those like him who have come near me?

We have failed him and those like him. Over and over after acts like these we hear, "This is not the time to talk about…." But if not now, when? If we have to wait some long length of time, we will never talk about it. The fact that we face this once every four or five days leaves no time for us to wait.

We have to talk. And we have to act as God's agents. We elect those who say they will change the laws and they will help those like this boy — but they don't. And then we elect them again. It makes no sense to me. How can God bear to watch what we are doing to each other? How can God not reach in and stop us? I don't know. But maybe God has tried — and we have not heard God speak to us.

I have prayed for all those who grieve and for all those who have had to go back into this school. But as I heard a man say on the radio, "We need more than prayers." So I ask God what my part in that "more" is. What more am I called to do? I don't know yet. For sure I don't know what you are called to do, but I think God calls each of us not just to care and to pray but to act, to "be the change we want to see" in the world.

Help us, O God, to hear your call. Help us to see how we are to be part of your work to heal your world and each of our towns. We ask this for the sake of all the dear ones in them for whom Christ died, that no more will have to die.

Mary Lou Redding

54
Is That God?

*S*amuel did not know the Lord: The word of the Lord had not yet been revealed to him.... The Lord came and stood there, calling as at the other times, *"Samuel! Samuel!"* Then Samuel said, *"Speak, for your servant is listening."* (1 Samuel 3:7, 10 NIV)

Those early years, I didn't know God. When I was a kid, we didn't go to church very often. When I was twenty-two, a friend sent me a book about God, but I couldn't grasp most of it. The words were long, with vague terms that I couldn't quite ever latch on to. But one idea *did* stick with me — God loves me, with a love that is pure, holy, and more than I had ever known in the past.

How could I learn more about this God of love? I sought a Christian friend who would not laugh at me and began to share: "I don't have a clue about who God is. And what about this Holy Spirit?"

My friend's clear words were like darts of truth that took aim at my heart: "Ask God to cast aside your sin and dwell in your heart." When I heard these words, I didn't pray them right away.

Lin (left) with twin, Patty Conti.

What if this is a fad? I thought. *I don't know much about God, but I bet if I ask God to be in charge of my life, He will hold me to that vow. Then what kind of a mess will I be in?*

After a bit, drawn by His love, I *did* choose to pray. Not sure of how to go about it, I read a phrase from the back of a Christian book. After every few words, I would pause and gaze up, to make it clear to God that I meant what I said. Since I was quite shy, I didn't tell my friend about my new walk with God. Only later, after a few weeks, did I learn how many Christians had been going to God for my sake.

Today, I find great joy in the way God prompts each heart to long for Him. No two take the same route. My twin and I don't just look alike; we talk alike, smile alike, and even think alike. Her kids can't tell her voice from mine on the phone! At times we even feel as if we are only one person. But we did not come to God by the same path. Pat was drawn to Him at a slow pace over a span of time, years in fact. On the other hand, once I knew who God is, my road was quick — with an exact, sure time I could point to when God began to tug at my heart.

I stand in awe of a God who views even twins who seem just alike as two souls, each apart from the other. He called to my twin and me just as He calls to each of us — in ways only He can and with a tune that each of us alone can hear.

Lin Daniels

Fictionalized non-fiction

55

The Un-Contemplatable

I stood on the beach in the most out-of-the-way place in the world — a place where many had lost their lives. And like them, I was alone — claimed by no one. I had, in short, lost my way.

Before the war, as part of the Kwajalein Atoll, the coral out crop known as Roi Namur had been two small knots of coral: Roi and Namur. After the Japanese lost, the Americans closed the small inlet and made them one. Based on the count of shell holes in each pill box, the fight had been fierce. It was easy to feel the fear. Both sides reeled from the loss of lives. Then, the worst that could occur did. The isle of Roi blew up. After that, all went quiet — no birds, no men in pain, no rapid-fire guns. 'near all on Roi were dead. The Marines had tossed a bomb into a cave full of Kamikaze Torpedoes. At the time, no blast had ever reached that level of sheer power and might.

It was here that I met Amelia. Yes, Amelia Earhart. She was in full color, not grey as in the old news reels. And I sensed that she knew how my heart ached for my kids. You see, my wife was done with me, and I could not stop it.

I had been told by my host that a pen with "AME" on it had been found here. It was thought to be Amelia's. As I stood in front of the jail cell in which she may have lived, I knew that Amelia was there with me. Do not ask me how; I just knew.

On the calm side of Roi Namur, Amelia and I saw a small nerf shark. Like us, she had no other place to be. I tried to ask Amelia why life couldn't be fair, but I knew she would not reply. Her being there was all I could ask of her.

The sun fell low as I made my way into the water, sat down,

and cried. I love the smell of salt and sand, but none of that was going to help. Amelia sat near, still quiet. The Pacific was warm, and a dark spot in my soul grew. I knew that I could just walk into the ocean, and no one would miss me. The waves sang to me; the lie grew, and I contemplated "the un-contemplatable."

For her part, Amelia stared out over the vast Pacific Ocean and took it all in, the way a lover would breathe in the one she loved. Then she looked me in the eye.

"It's going to be okay, Paul," she said. "You must stay aloft, even when the sun isn't there to show you the way," she said softly, "so as not to annoy the nerf shark." And then, the way a ghost would slip into the night, she was gone.

I knew she was right. The nerf shark had ceased her play and began to make her way toward the west. The tide rose, and the wind died. It was time to move on. I stood and felt the grip of the Pacific slip away. and the dark spot with it.

Who am I to argue with Amelia Earhart? I thought.

Paul Hinton

56
MY BOY

There they are...his old toys.
My eyes slide down as I walk past.
In that slice of time, I feel...
...a lump in my throat,
...a pang in my heart
...a tear in my eye.

I think on my boy of past years.
Rust has come to toy trucks and John Deeres,
New buds in spring come back,
Hot June suns beat down,
Fall leaves sail past,
Cold snows drive like knives.

Time flies on and we wait...
for a small child who will not
be back.
Where is my boy now?
The one who played all day in
the dirt...
...his load of rocks and sand
and worms,
...on their way to a new home.

He walks on to new things,
Cars and coins and girls.
And me?
I shine up the old toys...
for a new child...one day...
Who may come back and play.

KYLE AND HIS TOY TRUCKS

Wilma R. Vernich

57
IN HIS BOOK

Once a month I meet to pray with my friend Caroline. We talk about how kind God is to us, and we share many things — some of which tug at our hearts. We laugh, too. Caroline and I talk about good food, shoes with open toes, great nail color, and the beach. Fine books, our children and our husbands are also in the mix.

Once, when we had reached our time but not yet prayed, Caroline said we needn't worry or fret. With her Bible in hand, she found Malachi 3:16 and read aloud:

Those who revered the L<small>ORD</small> spoke with one another. The L<small>ORD</small> took note and listened, and a book of remembrance was written before him of those who revered the L<small>ORD</small> and thought on his name (NRSV).

We liked this verse so much that we chose to study the whole Old Testament Book of Malachi when next we

BECKY WITH CAROLINE BABCOCK

met. We read that God's people were in a very sad state. The pride of their priests had led them into sin of all sorts and shapes. Many of them put more trust in their wealth than in God. Some spoke harsh words about Him and said, "What good does it do to serve God?"

Yet, not all of God's people were in such a state of worry and doubt. Some still feared the Lord and thought on His name.

Some still had deep trust in Him. Some still spoke kind words about Him.

And God heard them and wrote them in His book.

While that was more years ago than we care to count, my friend and I agree that not much has changed since the Book of Malachi was penned. Verse after verse, book after book, age after age — God's family are still the same.

So is God. We read in Malachi 3:6 that He does not change. God still hears us.

And so, with a sweet peace in our midst, Caroline and I now read Malachi 3:16 each time we meet. We make sure to speak kind words about God even while we share what tugs at our hearts. We think this is a good way to fear the Lord — to think upon His name. We still talk about food, shoes, nail color, and the beach; books, children and husbands are still in the mix.

But when we meet to pray, we also think about God with His hand cupped to His ear. We like that He hears us even if we have yet to bow our heads. In our minds' eye, we see God smile as we talk about Him. And, we smile to think that we are in His book.

Becky Hitchcock

FICTION

58

RESCUE AT THE TELE-WINK GRILL

Like most nights, after all have gone, Julip walks up and down the Tele-Wink Grill's lot. This night, after what seems eons since folks began to take note, boss lady Wanda means to find out why. She creeps up and locks Julip in the beam of the car's lights.

"Have you gone slap silly?"

"Hey Wanda!"

Julip takes a few quick steps, bends to pick up some shiny thing, then puts it into a cup.

"I said are you crazy? Folks talk!"

"In a way I *might* be crazy!"

Wanda edges the car close to Julip's side. In a low, stern tone Wanda probes. "Pray tell. Why's that?" Julip's eyes light up. She takes a few quick steps and bends over to reach out of Wanda's sight. A "tink" rings from the cup. Julip pops up and starts off again.

At the Tele-Wink grill, there's been no change since Truman made the White House his home 40 years ago. The same hardwood booths rub folks the wrong way, and mangy metal fans still spew a hot wind when cool air makes the most sense. This is all why Julip still has a job.

Newer places set a high bar for one who works there. But a hole-in-the-wall like the Tele-Wink Grill has no bar. It's the right place for a gal with no job skills to speak of. Wanda took a chance on Julip a year back when Julip's man left to chase some flight of fancy he saw in an ad on the side of a bus. The story spread about town is that Julip can't have kids, and when she put the topic to adopt on the table, Ricky Wayne's reply was, "When pigs fly." Then, Julip took-in a child from Macon County Orphanage on a short-term basis. It was the last straw for the small town's 1986 sports hero.

Now folks think that time has taken its toll. The talk is, Julip's gone crazy. If it's true, that's one change the Tele-Wink Grill will *have* to make.

"Julip, we need to go in. *Now*."

Talk is slim at first. Then, Julip bursts out. "I just may be crazy but it's not the kind of 'crazy' you think."

"How's that?"

"It's crazy faith. Ya see, each night I try to hunt down a penny or two."

"Go on."

"My crazy faith is for a big house."

"A big house? It's just you and that child that never left."

"I want to take in more."

"Go on."

"Each night I pick up every penny I see. Yuh see, there are many a penny to find in this lot. It's the least of coins, and most don't stop for it. 'kinda like some of those Macon kids. At church, I place every penny into the plate and pray God will bless the gift. Yuh see, God makes more out of less."

"Well slap *me* silly!"

"See?"

"Darn right. We need a big jar in here. Each time folks pay, they'll put a penny in."

"Thank you, but no. To me, it means more to pick up from the ground what no one sees or cares about. Same as God does. Just give me time. You'll see what God will do."

Arm-in-arm, the two leave. One has a new lease on the job she holds. The other has a new sense of the God she left years ago.

Kenneth Avon White

59
Quilts and More Quilts

Each cloth is bright — red, orange, green, blue, and of course white — some plain, some plaid, some with stripes or dots. Such is my stash — those and more, with much to choose from. Even so, I never seem to find just the right shade for parts of a new quilt, so off I go to the craft shop to add a yard or two to my grand cache. Sew, shop, grow — sew, shop, grow and on it goes.

I love to quilt by hand with one stitch at a time — some big, some small. How does a sewer keep them even? Try as I might, they have a mind of their own. How did the gals in days of yore do it? Theirs look so exact!

What do I do wrong? I can blame the cloth — too thick, too thin. The tool I used to sew could be dull. My eyes might be tired, or the thread might fray. The cause I do not know. My quilts may not look the best, but each stitch does hold firm.

What do I learn as I quilt? Don't give up. A sure hand, a good eye, and grit make for fine work. If at first you don't do it right, rip it out and do it once more. Do your best.

Quilt Patricia made for her granddaughter

Each quilt is one of a kind, sewn with love and prayer. My hope is that it will be a gift to be kept for a long time.

I will make more quilts, some for new babes, some for those in my house and some for those who need the warmth of a quilt to know that a friend cares. Each time I sew, I thank God for this gift and for the joy it gives me.

And one day, each stitch may be part of a true line from start to end.

She seeks wool and flax
And willingly works with her hands.

Proverbs 31:13 NKJV

Patricia A. Earl

60
Maybe Next Time

"My name is Mary Webb," I told the woman at the front desk. "I've come to visit my mother, Kay Hunt."

"Yes. Sign the guest book, please." With a nod to a big room to one side, she said, "Mrs. Hunt is in there. This is their day to sing while a lady plays the piano."

I moved to the door of that room and stood there. I stared at each face under a thatch of white hair as they looked at me. Then each would turn back to the lady at the front of the room. But I couldn't find my own mom! Where was she?

Mary & her mom, Kay Hunt

I stood there so long that an aide came to me and said, "Mrs. Hunt is right there!"

No it isn't, or...could that frail woman be my mom?

She didn't look at all the same as the last time I had seen her. I went over to sit by her.

"Mom?"

Her hazel eyes met mine, but she didn't seem to know me.

"It's Mary," I told her.

"Mary? *My* Mary?"

Her bony hand stretched out to touch my face. The vast change in her made me want to cry, but I held back the tears. The last time I saw her, she had been in her own place. Now she was in this care home.

"Yes. I came from New Mexico to visit you."

"You drove to Oklahoma City to visit me?"

"Yes."

Could this be the mother of my youth, the one who would hold me when I had a fever and go with me to ball games at school? She didn't look at all like the one who baked and sewed while noisy storms slapped fat drops of rain on the glass panes of our home.

She moved her thin arm to grasp my hand and said, "I'm sorry."

"About what?" I asked.

"I haven't baked a thing for you!"

I laughed and cried at the same time, as tears rolled down my cheeks. This was the mom I knew after all!

"It's all right, Mom! I'm still full from lunch."

Her head moved in a nod. "Maybe the next time you come."

"That's right," I gave her hand a pat. "Maybe next time."

Mary Hunt Webb

61
FAITH, LOVE, MUSIC

If you drive down a small dusty Missouri road in the heat of mid-July, you will view acres of crops as far as you can see, with a barn or house that pops into view only once in a while.

CHURCH

In fact, you might miss a place that was once a busy farm town but which is now no more than a wide spot in the road. A sign off to the side still says "Indian Grove," but all that is left is a white church, still used, with well-kept graves in back — many of which hold names that have come up in tales told by Grandmother. We would leave roses, pray, and be sad at so many tiny graves.

INDIAN GROVE LANDSCAPE

At one time this church was the hub of daily life in this tiny town, but now it is open only for an hour or two on Sundays, with a visiting priest who says Mass for those who still like to come there best. My great-great-grandfather's home, near the church he helped build, is gone with no sign of it to be found; nor can his store be seen on the main road.

One-half mile down that road is a small house built by my great-grandfather. While once home to 14, one of them my grandmother, it now shows no sign of life. A huge tree in the front still gives shade to the well, their only source of water, and if you close your eyes you just might think you hear a laugh from a child as he plays in the yard. My great-grandfather loved music and would play flute and strings for the family while they sang. They, too, grew up to love these times filled with music and pass that love on to their own.

Family home

The road was once lined with other homes, but now only this one stands, and it looks frail — as if it will not stand long. Faith, love, and music were a big part of the life of that house and stayed a part of the lives of the siblings long after they left home. When you think of it, isn't that what lives with all of us through the years — faith, love, and music?

Marcy O'Rourke

About the Authors

Tabitha Abel (p. 14) is a retired nurse, midwife, and health educator and also teaches online. At the time of writing "Stop Thief," she was enjoying a mission trip to Papua New Guinea where she and her husband, Gary, were painting a mission house and providing First Aid and CPR instruction to flight-ground staff.

Shortly before that, they were in Kiribati assisting with dental clinics and a mission-school building project. Tabitha and Gary are both the youngest of five children and enjoy hiking, camping and eating healthfully. Tabitha was born in England but has made the USA her second home for 30-years. She can be reached at tabithaabel@yahoo.com.

Jeff Adams (p. 76) has contributed to 16 books and authored one, *Encouraging Words: Rebuilding Your Dreams*. He's written more than 1,200 articles. His work has been translated into almost three dozen languages in at least 100 countries, reaching an estimated 18 million people. He was once published by the editors of the *Wall Street Journal*. The San Diego Christian Writers Guild honored him as the 2007 Sherwood Eliot Wirt Writer of the Year. He is also a certified substantive editor and member of Christian Editor Connection.

Partially paralyzed after a basketball injury at age 16, blinded by a racquetball in 1982, and in 2001 briefly dead when his heart flatlined, Jeff believes in miracles. Jeff is a pastor, teacher, and speaker. He lives in Arizona with his wife, Rosemary. Those interested in booking speaking engagements can contact him at jeffadams@frontiernet.net.

Karen O'Kelley Allen (p. 57) has a passion for music, ministry, and dogs. On Sundays she plays the organ for her church at Meadow Brook Baptist church in Birmingham, Alabama where she and her husband of 35 years, George Parker (Parky), attend. On weekdays she works as a quality assurance manager in the area of cancer research at the University of Alabama Comprehensive Cancer Center. She enjoys spending vacations on the mission field at home and internationally.

A diagnosis of breast cancer inspired her to write her Bible study *Confronting Cancer with Faith* (www.confrontingcancerwithfaith.com), which has brought encouragement to people around the world. Karen enjoys speaking, singing, and writing and has published numerous articles and devotionals through LifeWay Christian Resources, Grace Publishing, and Christian magazines and newspapers such as *The Alabama Baptist*.

Sharon Atwood (p. 55) earned a B.A. from Birmingham Southern College and completed her master's in special education at the University of Alabama at Birmingham. Realizing that she wished to work with the elderly as well as children, she became a certified home health aide. To follow some of her true passions, she has also immersed herself in poetry, writing, and artistic expressions.

An active member of her local church, she enjoys participating in Bible studies in community settings. She is currently living her dream to share her story with the mental-health community as well as the community at large as an In Your Own Voice spokesperson for the National Alliance of Mental Illness. Her works have been published in all four books in the *Short and Sweet* series.

Adam Benson (p. 71) lives in North Carolina with his wife, Meghan, and their beagle, Charlie. He graduated from Furman University with a bachelor's degree in psychology and Duke Divinity School with a master's in divinity. He has worked at Duke Law School and as a youth minister and for five years served as a Young Life leader. He is in the process of being ordained as an Elder in the United Methodist Church and was just appointmented co-pastor at 1st United Methodist Church in Elon.

He loves the outdoors and spent two summers living and working in Yosemite National Park. He also loves to run, bike, write, play sports — golf and disc golf — and watch sports, movies, and TV shows on Netflix with his wife.

Lanita Bradley Boyd (p. 16) draws on years of teaching, church ministry, and family experiences for her freelance writing and speaking. She enjoys mentoring young women through Bible studies and planning spiritually uplifting events.

Lanita travels with her family and has been on mission trips lasting three-to-six-weeks each. On these trips to Brazil, Panama, Fiji, Malaysia, and Thailand, she offers free English lessons based on Bible stories. She also works locally to help new English speakers improve their language skills.

Lanita is married to Stephen Boyd — speaker, author, and minister. They live in Fort Thomas, Kentucky, where they serve at the Central Church of Christ. They have a son and daughter who brought to the family another daughter and son and four wonderful grandchildren. She can be reached at lanitaboyd@gmail.com.

Adora (Jenny) Calvert (p. 67) has always had a love for writing, but with church work and children, she had to put this on the back burner of her life. Now that she is older and her children are raised, she has rekindled this passion.

A contributing writer for dailyprayer.us under the link Daily Inspiration, Jenny has also had two devotionals published in *The Upper Room* magazine and has written many other devotionals she hopes to one day publish in book form. Her blog, Liberty Ladies Devotional, is available at www.libertayladiesdevotional.blogspot.com.

In her spare time, Jenny helps with the grandchildren, teaches piano lessons, plays in two bell choirs, and quilts.

Jeanetta Chrystie (p. 18) and her husband live in Springfield, Missouri. She is a distance Assistant Professor of Business Administration at *Southwest Minnesota State University*. Jeanetta has published more than 800 articles in magazines such as *Christian History*, *Discipleship Journal*, and *Clubhouse*. Her 150 newspaper columns appeared in the *Northwest Christian Examiner*, and she has contributed to anthology books and textbooks since the 1970s. She would like to publish, or self-publish, five chapbooks of poetry written by herself and her grandmother.

Jeanetta is a firm believer in spiritual journaling and prayer journaling, teaches Sunday School, and has a passion to write Bible studies and devotions. As a survivor of both polio (age 2) and cancer (age 22), she clings to God as her mainstay and seeks to fulfill His reasons for preserving her life. Learn more about Dr. Chrystie at www.ClearGlassView.com. Connect with her on Twitter:@ClearGlassView, LinkedIn: Jeanetta-Chrystie, and Pinterest: Jchrystie.

Karen Condit (p. 11) enjoyed a 25-year career as a Reading Specialist and is now pursuing her passion by writing for children. She especially loves testing her stories on her six grandchildren. She also writes spiritual memoir. Her latest project combines these interests in a series of short stories for children, with themes drawn from the disciplines of the spiritual life.

When not writing she enjoys gardening, kayaking, quilting, and connecting with friends for meaningful conversation — always with a good laugh, coffee, and chocolate.

Sharon Cook (p. 61) spent most of her life in California, happily moving with her husband to Arizona in 2006. Recently widowed, she is a mother of four, grandmother of seven, and great-grandmother of 13. Arizona is full of "snowbirds," but she is a "sunbird," escaping to the Arizona White Mountains each summer to avoid the Phoenix heat.

In between her obsessive quilting and reading, she is a speaker who gives destination lectures on cruise ships, presents her lecture series "Our Marvelous Brain," speaks at Christian Women's Connection, and teaches Bible studies. She is a writer and editor. Her book, *Windows on the World*, is available on Amazon.com or Kindle. She is currently working with her sister, a mother of four handicapped daughters, on a book about their family life.

Lauren Craft (p. 74) believes our Heavenly Father gives each of His children a purpose, and that fulfilling His plan is one of the greatest joys we can experience before reaching our eternal home. God has blessed Lauren with a journalism post in downtown Washington, D.C., where she has worked for ten years as a reporter and magazine editor. She has also been overjoyed to aid in Bible translation and share her hope in Jesus Christ on four continents.

Her writings have appeared in the books *Just Breathe*, *Let the Earth Rejoice*, *Breaking the Chains*, *Short and Sweet Too*, *Merry Christmas Moments*, and the magazines *Refresh* and *Living Real*. Lauren lives in Woodbridge, Virginia and is happily married to Thomas Craft. You can connect with her at www.laurencraftauthor.com.

After forty years, Lin Daniels (p. 110) retired from teaching physical education — all but one year serving at the elementary-school level. She and her twin sister are avid golfers and especially enjoy playing as partners. As such they negotiate over which identical clothing to wear but choose one item (usually a hat) to be different. It is essential to zig and zag as teammates, so they have to remain slightly dissimilar.

Recently, Lin has found a passion for pickleball – a game similar to tennis but played on a smaller court while using a whiffle ball. Her other interests include writing Christian devotions, working with youth at church, and preaching — when offered the opportunity. Lin gives thanks to God for the depths of His love as well as all the "surprises" He has graciously bestowed on her.

Jorja Davis (p. 20) is an award-winning writer and poet. She has also been a classroom teacher, Sunday school teacher and coordinator, librarian, Kappa Phi (Christian women's collegiate club) sponsor, and early-learning-center and church-youth director. All this and more were enabled by her husband Bill's career moves during a twenty-six-year Air Force career, and only three moves in the twenty years since he retired. Jorja now marks the block "retired" on demographic surveys.
Mostly that means waiting to see what God plans next.

She is the oldest of three sisters all of whom love and care deeply for their mother — just turned ninety — and for one another. They are all grateful for the grace their children bestow by wanting them to be involved with their grandchildren — the opportunity to pass on to another generation the grace they, in turn, received from their mother.

Karen deBlieck's (p. 33) writing reflects the tension of finding her identity and the sense of belonging she struggled with as a black American born in Japan and adopted by white Canadian missionaries. From a very young age, she found solace in putting her thoughts and feelings down on the page. Whatever she writes — whether in the form of a poem, short story, or novel — her pieces are charged with emotion and conflict.

She dreams of travelling through space and time, being sorted into a Hogwart's house, and finding her way to Neverland. When she's not writing or cooking for her hubby and four kids, she enjoys teaching teens about life and words. Check out more about Karen, the current novel she is working on, and her blog at http://karendeblieck.com/.

For over twenty years, Troy Dennis (p. 43) has been an ordained minister and chaplain. Musical, he sings and plays trumpet, bass, and acoustic guitar. Troy loves anything to do with the outdoors, including canoeing, photography, hunting, camping, and running. For some years, he and friends took an annual canoe trip to explore wilderness areas. The longest of these trips involved more than five miles of portages. Recently, he participated in a 30-mile running and canoeing endurance race.

Married since 1990, he and Jan have two grown children. Together, they lead worship in their church in Manitoba, Canada.

For forty years, Jon Drury (p. 93) has served as a pastor and also published over 400 articles and two books. He is a former Air Force pilot, and in addition to his first title *Lord I Feel So Small*, just published *BOU Pilot,* his account of flying as a transport pilot in the Vietnam War 1968-1969.

Jon began writing and publishing in 1992 when he attended Ethel Herr's *Introduction to Christian Writing* at Mount Hermon Christian Writers' Conference. Beginning with devotionals, he transitioned to articles, then books. In 1994, he began the Christian Writers Seminar that he directed for twenty-one years. The seminar is now West Coast Christian Writers under Susy Flory.

In 2012, at Mount Hermon, Jon received the David Talbott Special Recognition Award for leading the Christian Writer's Seminar for nineteen years.

Patricia A. Earl (p. 119) lives in Manotick, a small town on the edge of Ottawa, Ontario, Canada. As an army brat and army wife, she had the opportunity to experience many other parts of the world. Now, her husband, Brian, and she are enjoying retirement. She particularly likes to write, quilt, work in the garden, and help lead a Bible study in their home.

Patricia is the devotions editor for an e-zine called *Eternal Ink* which is published twice a month. For a number of years, she has been a member of Inscribe Christian Writer's Fellowship. She plays keyboard in her church praise team and sings in the choir. Patricia is also an elder on her church session. She and Brian are blessed with three married children, five grand-children and two great grandsons.

In 2004, Sharon (p. 94) married Mark Fincannon, a mighty man of God and casting director in the film business. God then opened the door for her to minister to women in that industry. The impact of those encounters continues to be life changing.

Sharon believes that God healed, redeemed, and purposed her previous pain and struggles for the good of others. She's brought those treasures to others for several years now by offering them wisdom, healing, encouragement, and purpose to help them fulfill their destinies. She loves having a front-row seat to watch what only God can do in their lives.

One of Sharon's faith-filled experiences is having been diagnosed and miraculously healed of breast cancer in 2013. Her blog was born out of that experience. It can be found at momentswithmeblog.wordpress.com.

From the time she was placed in a seventh-grade creative-writing class, Joanne Fleck (p. 78) knew that she really enjoyed writing. However, it wasn't until fairly late in life that she found a path toward pursuing this calling.

Then, once Joanne was finally able to get started on her first serious writing project, her work was slowed down while she and her husband cared for her father, who was suffering from dementia.

Although it seemed like a delay, Joanne could see God's hand in it. During that time, she learned much about writing skills that could improve the quality of her writing. If it weren't for the delay, her writing project wouldn't have been able to possess the same level of appeal.

Pat Gerbrandt (p. 32) enjoys reading, researching, and writing stories. Believing that everyone has a story, she encourages even non-writers to find a way of sharing their experiences. Genealogy helps her to piece together stories and to connect people. Pat is passionate about advocating for those who cannot speak for themselves.

For nearly ten years, she has served on the Board of Directors of a faith-based personal-care home. A member of both Manitoba Christian Writers Association and InScribe Christian Writers' Fellowship, Pat is grateful for the tremendous prayer support and the professional development they offer.

Walking and bicycling are her favorite forms of exercise. Pat and her husband have three grown children, all married, and seven grandchildren. She enjoys baking, table games, camping, tea, and reading with the grandchildren.

Pamela Groupe Groves' (p. 36) childhood included many family-centered activities, but her parents also encouraged developing independence and learning to entertain oneself. Pam and her friend Beckie definitely worked on both skills through their creative adventures in the neighborhood and beyond, many of which the mothers did not know about until the girls reached adulthood.

Pam's childhood helped prepare her for writing, teaching, and moving with her husband from Oregon's high desert to the coast and finally to the big city. All the while they were parenting six adopted children, four with special needs. Their life together was a little offbeat with unexpected twists and turns, including her husband's death at age 62 from a rare cancer, microcystic adnexal carcinoma. Through it all, they trusted that God was present in their lives.

As a speaker, published author, and storyteller, Carol Harrison (p. 82) is passionate about mentoring people of all ages and abilities to help them find their voice and reach their fullest potential. She shares from her heart, telling stories from real-life experiences and God's Word to encourage people and help them find a glimmer of hope no matter what the circumstances.

Carol believes we need to continuously grow in our walk with God and lives out her storytelling passion by speaking at women's events and retreats, Bible Camps, school assemblies and church events. Carol is a wife, mother of four adult children and grandmother to twelve. She makes her home in Saskatoon, Saskatchewan, Canada.

The blue-haired writer, Leah "LM" Hinton (p. 84), always has her nose in a book, whether she is reading it or writing it. She has been married to a big-city detective for over twenty years and lives in a suburb of Dallas, Texas. She and her husband have been blessed with two children, five rescue dogs, a bird, and a rescue horse — all named after her favorite characters in literature.

Leah writes both fiction and non-fiction and is fueled by highly caffeinated coffee and a never-ending faith in God. A country girl at heart, this homeschool mom and cancer wife loves sharing her struggles and blessings with others going through similar situations and firmly believes that faith is the best remedy for life's toils.

Paul Aaron Hinton (p. 112) is the son of a proper British mother and a Mississippi mud father. Never sure if he should aspire to be James Bond or a character from *Hee Haw*, Paul has worked in many "fields." He hopes his colorful — if not ADD — view of the world reaches those who have never been sure if God needs them. Thus, Paul's motto is Philippians 4:13. *I can do all things through Christ who strengthens me.*

Paul has served the Methodist church for over 20 years as a Lay Minister in both youth and contemporary worship. He and his wife, Cecily, have three children, plus a "Crazy Cat Lady" starter pack of four cats and two very big dogs.

Becky Hitchcock (p. 115) is a long-time judicial secretary who lives and writes in Old Clyattville, a farming community outside Valdosta, Georgia. Becky has lived on the farm all but six months of her entire life. She and her husband, Keith, are high school sweethearts and have two grown daughters.

Becky has always been fascinated with the written word, but she did not make writing a priority until her second brother passed away. Whether penning articles and prayers, or piddling with a work of fiction, Becky feels God smiling when she writes. She had rather write than talk. When not writing, she reads about writing and writers. She still makes time to sip tea, walk a beach, and search for vintage Blue Willow china. Though she is a self-professed tech-a-phobic, more of her writing may be found at www.sensitiveonpurpose.blogspot.com.

Craig Hodgins (p. 12) was born in small-town Ontario, Canada. His work in IT gave him the opportunity to travel to many parts of Canada and the United States as well as the United Kingdom and Europe. Craig has spoken to international audiences on technical subjects, has published two articles, and won Best Paper at a conference.

For 12 years, Craig served as an auxiliary member of the Ontario Provincial Police and is currently an officer in the Canadian Armed Forces, working with youth in the Royal Canadian Air Cadets. He is a part-time lay preacher at the small country church where he has been attending since before he can remember.

Craig and wife, Joanne, have three grown children and one son-in-law. He loves to read, write, travel, and learn new things.

Doris Hoover (p. 30) is a wife, mother, and grandmother. Since retiring from teaching, she travels between Florida and Maine where she spends as much time as possible outside enjoying the beauty of each location. By combining her love for nature with her reverence for God, Doris writes about the lessons the Lord teaches her.

When she's not writing, she's dancing hula or rhythm-and -blues line dancing. When she's not dancing, she's traveling to New Jersey to visit her three daughters, their husbands, and her four grandchildren who range in age from six to eleven.

Doris has won awards for some of her devotions. She's been published in several compilations and magazines. Her first book *Quiet Moments in The Villages, A Treasure Hunt Devotional* is available on Amazon.com.

Patricia Huey (p. 47) was born in the Pacific Northwest but was raised in the South. She began her teaching career after graduating from the University of Alabama. Throughout her career, the subject she most enjoyed teaching was creative writing. In 2015 she retired as director of Hill Creek Christian School in Mount Vernon, Washington — the school she founded in 1994. She serves as a consultant for Hill Creek Christian, offering educational therapy to students who struggle with learning deficits.

Currently Patricia is developing her writing ideas to point her readers to God. In her spare time, she enjoys gardening, writing, and bird watching outside by her pond. She also enjoys time spent with family, friends, and her two Labrador retrievers, Braveheart and Scout.

Sheila Humphrey (p. 99) resides in Alberta, Canada and is a member of the Airdrie Writer's Group. This group recently published their second volume of work — *Voice and Vision 2017*. The publication came about as a collaboration between the writers and artists of Airdrie and the surrounding rural community. Sheila's writing appears in this volume as well as in *Voice and Vision 2016*.

A retired teacher, Sheila is also an avid participant in National Novel Writing Month (https://nanowrimo.org/) and has just completed her sixth novel with this program. The inspiration has come from participation with the Airdrie Writer's Group. Members are supportive of each other's writing, and their encouragement has helped Sheila to explore her writing craft.

Sheila Humphrey is also a member of a couple of choirs and enjoys the exploits of her children and grandchildren.

Tina M. Hunt (p. 24) is an encouraging communicator, whether she's writing or speaking. She serves as Co-President of Word Weavers Northeast Ohio and a mentor for Word Weavers International.

Being the pastor of First Church of the Brethren in Ashland, Ohio gives Tina opportunity to use all her gifts and fulfill her purpose. The apostle Paul penned the verse that has guided her life: *"I want you woven into a tapestry of love, in touch with everything there is to know of God.*

Then you will have minds confident and at rest, focused on Christ, God's great mystery" (Colossians 2:2 MSG).

When not working at church, Tina can be found caring for her grandson or having coffee with a friend. Her reflections and devotions appear on her blog, www.PotOfManna.wordpress.com or on the writers' website: www.almostanauthor.com.

Liz Kimmel (p. 104) has been married for 38 years and is the mother of two and grandmother of four. She earned a BA in Elementary Education at Bethel College in Arden Hills, Minnesota.

Liz loves to write in such a way as to make learning fun for elementary students. She has published two books of Christian poetry and a grammar workbook. Her current project is a set of worksheets about the 50 U.S. states — created in order of statehood and incorporating math and language arts skills, in addition to lots of puzzles. She serves as the Communications Coordinator for her church, Bethel Christian Fellowship, in St. Paul, Minnesota. She serves as the Communications Coordinator for her church, Bethel Christian Fellowship, in St. Paul, Minnesota, and also writes for and is layout editor for their bi-monthly church publication.

Bob LaForge (p. 106) has been a Christian since 1977 when God showed him that when he is in control of his life it does not go well. He realized that he needed to give control to the one true Lord and Savior. Bob and wife, Toni, are raising twin daughters, Sarah and Danielle, who were born in 2006. At their church, Grace Bible Church, Bob oversees the bookstore and teaches Adult Sunday School. Toni sings in the choir and is on the Fellowship Committee and their daughters are in AWANA and American Heritage Girls.

Bob has written three books: Contemplating the Almighty which discusses who and what God is, *Developing Great Relationships*, and *The Tempter Comes* which is a novel about evil that comes to an isolated town. Bob's website can be viewed www.disciplescorner.com.

Marcia Lee Laycock (p. 97) is the author of *One Smooth Stone* for which she won the Best New Canadian Christian Author Award. The sequel, *A Tumbled Stone,* was also short-listed for a Word Award and has garnered excellent reviews. Marcia's four devotional books are listed among her award-winners, and she has contributed to several anthologies including all of the Hot Apple Cider books. Her most recent release is *Celebrate This Day*, a devotional for special occasions.

Marcia is a sought-after speaker for women's events and writers' conferences. She lives with her favorite pastor in Central Alberta Canada. She can be found on the web at her website marcialeelaycock.com, Amazon, and Smashwords.

Alice H. Murray (p. 73), a proud member of a military family, lives in Florida where she has practiced adoption law (domestic non-related infant adoptions) for over 25 years. Alice is an officer and board member of the Florida Adoption Council and of Hope Global Initiative.

While being a lawyer is her profession, Alice's passion is writing. Alice has written articles for legal professional magazines as well as for her local paper and a missions' magazine; she also won

an American Bar Association haiku contest. Alice had a non-fiction piece published in *Short and Sweet* (the first book in the *Short and Sweet* series). In the near future, she hopes to have two books published — one a humorous devotional book and one a look back at her career as "Boss of the Babies" doing adoption work.

Suzanne Dodge Nichols (p. 96) grew up in Gulf Breeze, Florida. During high school, she discovered the rewarding discipline of writing. Through the years, she has found creative expression in almost every genre of the printed word. She especially enjoys blending words and art in ways that can both delight and challenge the observer.

Through her church, she leads a scripture-memory and Bible skills program for older elementary children called "Bible Drill." Her years as program director have led her to develop a three-cycle curriculum for older children. More recently, she added a companion curriculum for younger elementary children: a foundational program she named "Bible Basics."

Suzanne makes her home in Hartselle, Alabama with Roger, her husband of 41 years. They have three children and seven grandchildren who live *much* too far away.

Marcy King O'Rourke (p. 123) grew up in a medium-sized Missouri town where she kept finding relatives at every turn. This began a life-long interest in genealogy, and modern technology has sent her on an ancestor hunt with great success — leading her to write private genealogy books and narratives of their travels.

After high school, Marcy moved to San Diego, California where she earned a B.A. in English literature and later married her college sweetheart, Chuck, reared three daughters, and currently resides in a small town in Northern California. She worked in teaching for several years but found her real career love in human resources, retiring as a senior analyst. Now she enjoys babysitting for her third grandchild, which she has decided is the best job ever — with all the fun but little of the responsibility.

Debra Pierce (p. 88) lives in Auburn, Massachusetts with her husband, David. She holds an Associate Degree in Animal Care from Becker College in Leicester, Massachusetts and a Bachelor of Arts degree in English from Worcester State College in Worcester, Massachusetts. In 1999, Debra left a banking career to pursue her life-long dream of working with animals by starting a pet-care business.

Debra is a voracious reader and enjoys writing devotionals, several of which have been published by *The Upper Room*. Her other interests are gardening, birdwatching, walks in the woods, and visiting museums. She was a volunteer for Mass Audubon, a wildlife volunteer at a nature/science museum, and most recently, ministry leader for her church's garden ministry. As Debra approaches retirement, she looks forward to traveling with her husband and devoting more time to her writing.

Shelley Pierce (p. 69) is a pastor's wife, mother to four, grandmother, and author. Playing with the grandkids is her favorite way to spend a day. She also enjoys her day job, serving as Director of Preschool and Children's Ministries at Towering Oaks Baptist Church in Greeneville, Tennessee.

Her writing includes children's curriculum with *LifeWay Kids*, a column in *Christian Online Magazine*, contributions to *The Upper Room*, *Power for Living*, *Guideposts The Joys of Christmas*, *The Mighty Pen*, and *Stupid Moments*. Her middle grade novel, *The Wish I Wished Last Night*, has just been released.

Shelley chooses to look at the bright side of life, believing that God can be trusted to keep His promises. To her, difficulties in life — such as a son deployed in a war zone — are all opportunities to grow in faith and depend on God to meet needs. Check out her weekly blog at shelleypaperbackwriter.blogspot.com.

Karma Pratt (p. 27) is a Christian communicator who loves words almost as much as she loves God. As a writer and speaker with a background in professional communication, she is smitten with big words. *Short and Sweet Too* has challenged her to find joy in the mono-syllabic. Karma writes primarily poetry and non-fiction, although journaled prayers are also high on her list of writing accomplishments. She is a monthly contributor to the InScribe Writers Online blog. Someday she would love to author a Christian graphic novel.

Karma has worn many labels in her life but follower of Jesus, wife to Les, and mom to Corin and Kalliste are by far her favorites. She writes from the golden house in Northeastern British Columbia. You can connect with her online at www.redraincoatcreations.com or on Facebook.

Frank Ramirez (p. 42) shares three adult children and six grandchildren with Jennie, his wife of 43 years. They share their home with three dogs. Frank was born in California, but as a Navy brat spent much of his childhood in several states. He graduated from LaVerne College in California and Bethany Theological Seminary, at the time located near Chicago. He has been a pastor in the Church of the Brethren since 1979, serving churches in California, Indiana, and Pennsylvania.

Frank is a prolific writer, an avid reader, and a beekeeper. His favorite authors include Shakespeare, Tolkien, Lewis, Rex Stout, Samuel Beckett, and Saki. He owns two much-used editions of the Oxford English Dictionary. He reads Biblical Hebrew and Greek. Frank lives near Nappanee, Indiana.

Mary Lou Redding (p. 108) earned a degree in English Literature and a graduate degree in Rhetoric and Writing. After teaching basic composition and writing for pre-professional majors on the college level, she came to work for the international daily devotional magazine *The Upper Room*, for whom she taught at writers' conferences nationally and internationally. The assignment that led to the essays in this book grew from the effective writing workshops she taught for colleagues.

After thirty-three years with *The Upper Room* — she retired from her position as Editorial Director. In retirement, she has rediscovered the joys of having free time. She loves being more available to her family, especially in being part of the early years of a surprise grandchild. She is working on her eleventh book in a meandering, grandmotherly sort of way and dreaming about her twelfth.

Reba Rhyne (p. 45) is the pen name of Reba Carolyn Rhyne Meiller. She was raised in the western foothills of the Great Smoky Mountains, where her roots are firmly established.

Three-quarters of a century have passed since she was born. During this time, she was married for twenty-five years, had a daughter, and established a business as an on-site consultant, prototyping upholstered interiors for the marine industry.

During her months on the road, she wrote one-sheets about her travels. After attending several writing conferences, she expanded her scribbling. Her first novel, *Butterfield Station*, is available at Amazon, your local bookstore or Kindle. Another, *My Cherokee Rose,* is in the works.

For sixty years, she's been a Christ-follower who believes her responsibility is to follow the Great Commission found in Matthew. Contact her at rebarhyne@gmail.com.

After graduating from local schools and the University of Redlands, Susanna (p. 40) married Robert L. Robar. Robert, a retired Los Angeles City Fire Captain II, and Susanna, a retired Spanish teacher, have five children: two children are with the Lord; three adult children and four grandchildren live in Southern California.

Through her ministries, *RapeSpeaksOut!*, Susanna uses written materials, workshops, seminars, and short-term courses to educate parents, teachers, pastors and other child caregivers about sexual violence, child safety, and human sex trafficking.

For her efforts to help heal victims of sexual violence and prevent more children from becoming such victims, she received the Inaugural Cottey College Alumnae Hall of Leadership and Social Responsibility Award.

Tony Roberts (p. 86) was born in Southern Indiana. He graduated from Hanover College in English and theology and earned a master's degree from Louisville Presbyterian Seminary. He served 20 years in pastoral ministry with churches in Illinois, Pennsylvania, and New York. Now retired, he spends most of his time writing, podcasting, and visiting his family. Tony is delighted to have four children and three grandchildren.

Tony has written for publications such as *CT Pastors*, *Presbyterians Today*, *The Upper Room*, *devozine*, and *These Days*. His spiritual memoir, *Delight in Disorder: Ministry: Madness, Mission* is a reflection on serving as a pastor while battling bipolar disorder. His recent work can be found at delightindisorder.org. His new project is co-producing a podcast on faith and mental health called "Revealing Voices."

After dabbling in several careers throughout her adult life, Dottie Rogers (p. 53) is now happily retired. She is a graduate of Huntingdon College, Scarritt College, and the University of South Alabama. She was blessed to spend twenty years in the areas of local church Christian education and university campus ministry. She then had many rewarding years as a professional counselor in several settings.

She now enjoys hanging around the house with her husband Ken and their dog Shep. They live near the gulf coast where gardening is a twelve-month project. She also loves to read, cook, write, and teach adult Bible study. After fifty years of discipleship, she is still learning to follow. Although a reluctant disciple, she is always amazed at God's grace and guidance.

Sue Rosenfeld (p. 103) loves combining her analytical and creative strengths for great communications projects and fun events. An experienced coordinator, instinctive administrator, skilled presenter, and published writer, Sue delights in bringing ideas and words to life. She also enjoys singing, reading, entertaining, being at the water, and traveling.

A professional writer for over two decades and the founder and president of Rosenfeld Communications, Sue has produced a body of work that includes nonprofit public relations pieces, corporate communications, book contributions, and articles. Over the years, her writing, speaking, jobs, and volunteering have crossed a wide range of industries and venues. Sue holds a Bachelor of Science degree in Occupational Therapy from the University of Kansas; is a member of Toastmasters International; and is a homeschooling mom. Contact her at rosenfeldcommunications@gmail.com or https://linkedin.com/in/suerosenfeld.

Michelle Ruschman (p. 51) considers herself blessed to be the wife of Mark and mother of Marianne. The Florida panhandle is where they call home. There Michelle works as a jewelry artisan, an artist, and a part-time preschool teacher. She is best known for her original jewelry line, Beautifully Broken, one-of-a-kind dichroic glass crosses she fires in a kiln in her garage, as well as jewelry featuring Baybayin, the original writing system of the Philippines.

Michelle does most of her writing in the middle of the night. She loves the tranquility of those dark hours, claiming it's the only time her mind is finally quiet enough to receive inspiration from the Lord. Michelle writes mainly for her blog, *The Devotions of a Prodigal Daughter*, but is now exploring other publication opportunities as well.

Carol Schafer (p. 101) has authored three children's storybooks: *Lorenzo's Incredible Leap: A Story of Courage*; *Grison, the Grumpy, Grouchy Island Goat: A Story of Healthy Choices*; and *Cloddia's Desert Dance: A Story of Finding Your Place*. Each of these stories tells about an animal from a country Carol has visited: a llama from Peru, a goat from Haiti, and a dromedary from Israel.

Carol's career as an academic editor spanned a stretch of twenty-seven years, during which time she edited undergraduate course materials in a wide range of disciplines. Now retired, Carol has resumed her writing and publishing interests. She has recently been published in a Christmas anthology and in *Short and Sweet Too*. She lives in Alberta, Canada.

Leslie Neal Segraves (p. 25) is the co-founder and co-director of 10/40 Connections, a mission organization that seeks to cast hope to unreached peoples so that they hear, experience, and then multiply the Good News of Jesus in their own neighborhoods. Since its founding, 10/40 has helped rescue and restore hundreds of women from trafficking, fed and educated hundreds of at-risk children, planted multiplying house churches among over 70 unreached people groups, installed scores of water wells, and promoted curriculum and teaching that advocates for both women and the unborn.

Leslie is a motivational speaker whose greatest passion is to see the Great Commission finished in her lifetime. In 2017, Leslie and her husband, Chad, released *Engaged in Love and War: Awakening Commitment and Courage*. With their three children, they reside in Southeast Asia.

Writer and illustrator E.V. Sparrow (p. 63) enjoys spending time with her new husband and young grandchildren and serving as caretaker for her mother. Her favorite activities are hiking, kayaking, and creating art. During her years as a muralist, E.V. loved painting whimsical designs in children's rooms. Her current illustration projects, in watercolor and pen, depict the joy of life and relationships.

Prayer, worship, and ministry are vital to E.V. She led prayer teams and small groups in Divorce Care, Women's, and Singles' Ministries; and sang with a worship team and several choirs. E.V. is a member of Inspire Christian Writers and the Society of Children's Book Writers and Illustrators. Her passion is writing short stories of freedom, hope, and love. Her favorite subjects are interpersonal relationships and God's miraculous interactions with His people.

Pastor and recently retired USAF chaplain Jack Scott Stanley (p. 49) has been called to minister to troops in central California, Alabama, Washington D.C., Las Vegas, northern Italy, Oxford, England, and in a deployed setting to South West Asia, Iraq, Afghanistan, and many others that will have to remain unnamed. His first book, *Stand Strong: Spiritual Resilience the Ephesians Way*, was published in 2012, and he is a weekly columnist for his local paper. For 27 years Jack has been married to a teacher of British literature who helps him improve his writing skills. They have a daughter just in college and a son just out of it, both who publish blogs. He has performed as a musician around the world, and enjoys writing, sports, the arts, and all that God makes beautiful.

Kay Marshall Strom (p. 90) is the author of 42 published books. Her writing includes numerous articles, Sunday School and DVBS curriculum, books for children, compilation entries and meditations (including several versions of the NIV devotional Bibles, and *The Bible for Today's Christian Woman*). Kay has also written TV and movie scripts. While most of her books are non-fiction, she also has two fiction trilogies, one set in 18th century Africa, the other in India, following one family throughout the 20th century. Three books have received awards, including two topping the Library Association Booklist.

In addition to her writing, Kay is an in-demand speaker. Her work as a 21st century abolitionist takes her around the globe where she does research and speaks out against social injustice, especially modern-day enslavement.

Jewell Utt (p. 38) is a freelance writer and conference speaker. Her passion is to encourage women through the Word of God. Understanding the demands of life, she presents retreats that promote rest, change, and renewal. "Refreshment for the Servant's Heart" is one of her popular retreat themes. Jewell considers seeing women revived for their journey to be a great reward.

For over twenty years, Jewell has served in church leadership with a focus on teaching and outreach. She is the director of a community food pantry and the women's-ministry leader at her church. She and her husband live in a serene mountainous area. They have three married sons and enjoy playing with their first grandson. To read her devotions or book a retreat, visit her website at: www.jewellutt.com.

Wilma R. Vernich (p. 114) writes with compassion as a mother of two and a farmer's daughter. Learning on the knee of her father and through Scrabble games with family, Wilma went on to study journalism in college — infatuated with the power of prose. Although she has not written her book yet, Wilma often expresses her innermost yearnings through poetry and desires to encourage people in her meditation contributions to *The Upper Room*.

Besides her husband's claim that she makes good homemade bread, Wilma's other claim to fame probably puts her in the minority of people who still enjoy communicating through "snail mail." Wilma lives outside Nashville, Tennessee where she can see pretty sunsets and prefers to be outside any day — whether it's working in the yard, waterskiing on a lake, or riding her bike.

Michelle Walker-Wade (p. 80) is an author, speaker, teacher, professional in adult education and workforce development, and ordained minister. Michelle earned her bachelor's degree in liberal studies and business communications from Holy Names University and a master's in organizational leadership from Trevecca Nazarene University.

For more than twenty years, she has served in various leadership roles in church ministry and public education. For several years, Michelle and her husband co-pastored a small church in Modesto, Caliornia where she grew very passionate about mentoring followers of Christ to take leadership roles in the community and the marketplace. In May of 2017, Michelle published her debut book, *The Discipline of Kingdom Advancement*, in which she provides insight on how we can apply the teachings, motivations, and leadership style of Christ in our personal lives, churches, and communities.

Karis Waller (pp. 65, 66) lives in Elkhorn, Nebraska and enjoys teaching tiny miscreants (preschoolers) as well as writing poetry. She comes from a large, happy family of six children, where she inherited her unique sense of humor.

When she is not writing or corralling small children, she enjoys hanging out with her family, friends, and boyfriend; reading; baking; or binging food shows on Netflix. She is currently involved in Wordsowers writing group in Omaha, Nebraska, and her goal is to write her own book of poetry. Her favorite poets include Sarah Kay and Shel Silverstein. A favorite quote is: *"God is in the midst of her, she shall not be moved; God will help her when the morning dawns."* (Psalms 46:5-6 NASB).

Mary Hunt Webb (p. 121) is a recovering educator with a master's degree in adult education and workplace training and a bachelor's degree in Spanish. Her recovery is not going well since she teaches American Sign Language and supervises volunteers at her church. Mary has taught Spanish, English as a Second Language, and math. She specialized in assisting students to overcome life's challenges and attain career goals.

In order to reach those outside the classroom, Mary has written for various secular and Christian publications, including *Woman's Day* and *The Upper Room*. She was a professional consultant for *The Art of Helping* by Lauren Littauer Briggs and for *Love Extravagantly* by Marita Littauer and Chuck Noon. Mary and her husband own a consulting firm, Heart Works. Her husband is the webmaster for their website, www.maryhuntwebb.com.

Kenneth Avon White (p. 117) is an aspiring writer whose first publishing credit was for a devotional in *The Upper Room* magazine. He is also published in the first three books of the *Short & Sweet* series. Ken's professional background includes work in radio and television advertising, public relations, and corporate communications. He dreams of making writing his career; but in the meantime, he is grateful for the clock he punches.

For years, Ken lived in Nashville, Tennessee where he enjoyed the local music scene, theatrical shows, and art exhibits. Also high on his list there was dining out with a cast of characters — otherwise known as close friends — who have all been warned that most likely they will find themselves in one of his stories someday. He left Nashville to start a new job as a senior change-management consultant in Charlotte, North Carolina.

Karen Woodard (p. 59) is a homemaker, wife, and mother of five who enjoys reading, writing Christian poetry and devotions, crocheting prayer afghans, and serving on the food committee at her church.

Since her son's accident, she has wanted to share with others the story of the miraculous healing power of God that her family experienced through Ben's traumatic brain injury. He has made a full recovery and is now living the normal, active life of an 8-year-old. Karen has found that with God there is always hope, and we never walk alone no matter what trials we face. She wrote this story hoping to inspire others to trust in God. She firmly believes that although we don't always receive the outcome we desire in our trials, God never fails to supply what we need to see us through.

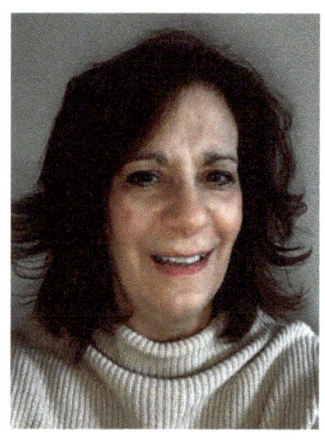

Andrea Woronick (p. 22) lives in New England with her husband, Michael, and her dog Rupert. She received a master's degree in biology and worked in medical research for several years until her two children were born.

At that time, she chose to stay home to raise her children and then began volunteering at their schools and in her church. For fifteen years she worked as the Director of Faith Formation at her church — creating, overseeing, and teaching programs for children and adults. She has since resigned her position and spends her time volunteering at a non-profit medical children's charity and at her church.

Andrea enjoys playing the piano, reading, gardening, traveling, and taking long walks with Rupert. She loves to write and hopes to continue to pursue this passion.

Susan Cheeves King

For over 23 years, Susan Cheeves King has served with *The Upper Room* a daily-devotional magazine that reaches millions of readers in more than 100 countries. One of her greatest joys in her role as Associate Editor has been representing *The Upper Room* each year by teaching at several of 23 different Christian writers' conferences in the U.S. and Canada. Her professional life also included teaching English and feature-writing classes at Lipscomb University, Biola University, and Abilene Christian University for a total of over 27 years. Early in her career, she served as book editor and radio-program producer/on-air talent for The Institute of Scriptural Psychology, wrote magazine features as a freelance writer, and functioned as a seminar facilitator in leadership and group dynamics. Susan and husband, Joe, live in Nashville, Tennessee, and have three grown children and two young grandchildren.

www.ingramcontent.com/pod-product-compliance
Lightning Source LLC
Chambersburg PA
CBHW042128160426
43198CB00021B/2943